D1736442

Marcy Goldman is a cookbook author, master baker and host of www.BetterBaking.com.

Library and Archives Canada in Publication

ISBN 978-1-927936-30-6 Print Book
ISBN 978-1-927936-31-3 EBook

Goldman, Marcy
The Newish Jewish Cookbook

Other Books by Marcy Goldman

Marcy Goldman is a cookbook author, master baker and host of www.Betterbaking.com. Her publishing imprint is River Heart Press. In addition, she has published traditionally with Random House U.S. and Canada, Doubleday, Broadway Books, Ten Speed Press and Oxmoor House.

Best Bagels, The Baker's Dozen, Volume Three, 2018 River Heart Press
Best Biscotti, The Baker's Dozen, Volume Two 2017 River Heart Press
Best Holiday Cookies, The Baker's Dozen, Volume One 2017 River Heart Press
The 10th Anniversary Edition of Treasury of Jewish Holiday Baking, 2017 River Heart Press
The Baker's Four Seasons, 2014, River Heart Press
A Passion for Baking, 2014 River Heart Press
Love and Ordinary Things, 2014 River Heart Press
When Bakers Cook, 2013 River Heart Press
A Treasury of Jewish Holiday Baking, 2007 Whitecap Books
The New Best of Betterbaking.com, 2007 Whitecap Books

Library and Archives Canada Cataloguing in Publication

Goldman, Marcy

Baking 2. Jewish

The *Newish* Jewish Cookbook

Over 140 Recipes for Holidays and Everyday

Marcy Goldman

River Heart Press
Montreal, Canada

Dedication

Dedicated with love to the women who taught me how to cook: my mother Ruth Ilieff Goldman, my Aunt Helen Goldman Miller, my grandmother Annie Goldman, and my mother-in-law, Shirley Posluns. It is also dedicated to my maternal grandmother Iliena Ilieff who taught me how to bless the bread and light the candles.

To everyone and anyone who appreciates the joy of gathering at the table and welcoming family, friends and newcomers

To my three sons, Jonathan, Gideon and Benjamin: you make ordinary days feel like holidays and simple foods taste like a feast. It must be the spice that love adds.

Contents

Chapter Nine: Fish 157

Chapter Ten: Vegetarian Dishes 171

The Newish Jewish Cookbook?

There's a meme about the Jewish grandmother, relentlessly pushing her children and grandchildren to eat, eat, eat! She makes far too much; the food is fatty and hardly 'healthy 'or even current; it's changeless in its tradition (but no one complains). But consider that she is this way because after years of oppression and starvation, the cultural expectation-turned-impulse to feed her family has become ingrained in her DNA.

Write the Cookbook *You* Want or How to Make a Better Knish

Many books, including cookbooks, come into being because the author didn't find the book they wanted already written. Part inspiration and part frustration is the less-than-artistic but equally important impetus behind many a great novel as well as a great cookbook. It comes from that school of thought that says: if you want something done right (or as you want) then do it yourself. This is *exactly* why I wrote my first book, *A Treasury of Jewish Holiday Baking*. At the time, I simply didn't see the book *I* wanted anywhere in the marketplace. Now, more than a few years have passed since I published my first cookbook, and here I am again, happily writing the Introduction to the counterpoint to my Jewish baking book, *The Newish Jewish Cookbook*. I wrote this book for the very same reason: the book I wanted didn't exist. Now, as I did then, I realized someone had to do it. I volunteered, and it's been a wonderful project to sign up for, not the least has been the joy of working with my volunteer testers who not only made each recipe perfect but infused the recipes with their lively energy and warm presence.

Over the years, I loved using my own first baking cookbook for all my Jewish baking, both daily things like challah and bagels, but especially the holiday foods. But when it came to *cooking*, my recipes were scattered about. Like so many of us, I had recipes in my head or jotted down in folders bulging with Word file print-outs. I also have always browsed recipes online as well as kept up with new Jewish cookbooks and trends to keep abreast of the appetizing changes in Jewish food. Certainly, I had no shortage of recipes but like most foodies, my recipe 'stuff' was all over the place and like many foodies, I love a great cookbook. Cookbooks have an anchoring sense to them. They're admirably solid and comprehensive, i.e. something to refer to, to hold in hand and to mess up with chicken soup and brisket gravy stains. To me a cookbook is a cohesive experience. At best, a cookbook is like being with a friend. Who wouldn't want to spend time with a friend in the kitchen?

Of course, there are already a great many Jewish cookbooks out there and truly inspired new Jewish cookbooks are being published all the time and most promise that hook of novel or original ways with the same old. But in the last few years and recently, the more I looked around, the more I noticed none had the 'everything' that I wanted in my own book. There are books on the new Israeli cuisine and Sephardic Jewish food. There are cookbooks that show you how to make innately non-kosher things (lobster, and other seafood, mixing milk with meat ingredients) kosher. Then there are the books that illuminate the tricks to making kosher foods and classic recipes 'lite' or lighter, and healthier as well as gluten-free kosher, vegetarian and vegan kosher, and there are homegrown family cookbooks that capture one family's memories and food as well as books on what has been termed Yiddish cuisine and/or deli favorites. I appreciate all those approaches, but for the book of *my* dreams? I wanted a book with *all* of this: the different spices of global Jewish food as well as the newer flavours, the hallmark and definitive recipes of diverse Jewish cultures, the lighter approaches to classics, as well as classics deconstructed to be authentic but (last but not least) easier. Now we have Instant Pots, spiralizers and electric shredders; on the shtetl we had mortars and pestles; a lot has changed! I also wanted to create a book with a pervasive teaching voice, a friendliness and embracive tone that welcomes any and every one to this type of cuisine because I love sharing. It's what I do both as a mother, a chef and as a writer. Admittedly, this is a lot of ground to cover but I love big adventures with big mountains to scale! And there is no bigger mountain to scale, in culinary terms at least, than the one called Jewish Cuisine.

A Jewish cookbook can be almost considered a history book – a history of 5700 years of happiness and sorrow. Jewish cooking is truly a melting pot. It has tasted the spices of Italy, the herbs of the Slavic countries, the tender lamb of Israel and the goulash of Hungary and Middle Europe.

Credit: Paul Grossinger, son of Jennie Grossinger, from the introduction of *The Art of Jewish Cooking*

So, what is Jewish food?

Open up just about any book on Jewish cuisine and chances are you'll find the question: "So what is Jewish food?" I smile because that question, by implication, illustrates how typical (and frequent) the question and how complex the answer.

Jewish food has a few distinguishing elements including first and foremost the observance of Kashrut aka the Jewish dietary laws, the seasonal calendar (Shabbats, new moons et al), which is also tied to Jewish history. The history of the Jewish people birthed the Jewish holidays with their accompanying food symbols. This morphed into the cuisine of a people who wandered the globe, bringing the taste of the homeland with them, and their customs, and mixed them up with the flavours of wherever they settled.

Another dimension to Jewish food and one it shares with all cultural cuisines is the regional availability of food, both geographically or regionally, as well as just simply, what is commonly available to a community at its own marketplace. One matches up one's needs and tastes to what is available, utilizing what is abundant, adapting when something is not.

The fourth influence, closely related to the proceeding one, and one that really accounts for the ever-evolving possibilities and new traditions in the Jewish kitchen, is its heritage of multi-cultural-ism. History recounts the trek of the Jewish people as they wandered for generations and settled in so many different lands. In essence, Jewish cuisine is the original Fusion Cuisine. Innovative, adap-tive Jewish homemakers adopted the new and strange foods and culinary ways of new communities and cultures, so different from their biblical homeland. As the newcomers birthed first, second, third and fourth generation home cooks, the velocity of Jewish food innovation increased exponen-tially – all the while adhering to the tethers of the Jewish holidays and the laws of Kashrut.

This food of Jewish wanderers who schlepped their dietary code and holiday food symbols is to me more of a weave than that melting pot metaphor. If you browse the Internet and cook-books, you'll see a blur of what is "Jewish' or Israeli, Persian, Palestinian and you name it. Things get adapted and twisted in creative turns. In the end, the threads are still identifiable but the food weave that results is more than the sum of its parts.

If you tabulate this impressive equation: a unique dietary code, holiday and historical traditions, indigenous ingredients & seasonal availabilities, a flair for (induced) cultural cross-fertilization and adaptation, you can understand how diverse that simple term, Jewish cuisine, really is. To say it's diverse is actually an understatement. It's also undisputedly rich, creative and unlimited. It also has a culinary DNA that is immutable. Jewish cuisine, like the lively culture it comes from, can take a lot of pulling and stretching, alterations, additions and re-interpretations (over 5000 years in fact). In the end, despite the liberties taken and inventiveness infused, it still has that anchoring note of authenticity that all soul food has. It reverberates with a special something that echoes through your stomach to your very spirit.

What is 'Newish Jewish' Cuisine?

So that's what Jewish cuisine is but what's 'newish- Jewish" cuisine? If you search the Internet, you will indeed, as I did, come across the term 'newish-Jewish' and it's a great turn of phrase to describe exactly what this book is about. *Newish* (versus new) means: a *little* new, a little different but all in all, not so overhauled that's it's no longer recognizable. I think when you go too far in service to innovation you run the risk of severing too many roots and you lose some visceral ties to the original mother ship. In doing this a whole cuisine might lose its bottom line content.

The other part of 'newish Jewish' is the *Jewish* of course. Considering the Jewish people have wandered from country to country and somehow retained a food heritage implies an evolving diversity but the same steady anchor, albeit two-fold anchor.

For one, Jewish cuisine implies that the recipes offer an adherence to the Jewish laws of kashrut. Secondly generally Jewish food, even in a subtle way, uses foods or ingredients that are related Jewish table occasions, whether they are a simple Shabbat supper or a festive Passover feast because Jewish food and Jewish holidays are integrally linked by food symbols. This baseline enduring food tenet is really pivotal. If you make things 'kosher' but there's no particular connection to Jewish culture either in food roots or history of cuisine culture, then it is indeed kosher but not memorably (to me) Jewish. Recipes tell a story and perpetuate an evolving history. Those great new kosher recipes are of incredible value and inspiration, especially for cooks wanting new and fresh twists that are coincidentally kosher. But to be clear, 'kosher sushi' or a 'kosher' (mock) ham (smoked tofu perhaps) and cheese (vegan cheese) are indeed *kosher* but not particular *Jewish* in cultural terms. To me these are creative and serviceable recipes but they're not culturally indicative of the great tradition, especially when we consider the timeless food symbols and dishes that show up on the menu of the major Jewish holidays.

You Don't Have to Be Jewish to Enjoy Newish Jewish

Just to be clear and embracive, anyone can enjoy this food; you don't have to be Jewish to be curious, enjoy great, healthy, interesting food. This is really not only 'newish' Jewish, this is a book for everyone! From my personal stance as well as from my perch as a chef, I prefer things that push the envelope forward both in terms of easier techniques, or something that reflects a more contemporary palate. Sometimes you discover a more definitive or unique way to cook up a classic which ensures that it will have an even more sustainable place on the Jewish table.

I also happen to like a diverse palette of spice and herbs so marrying a few Jewish flavor approaches under one roof also has its appeal. I'm also a fan of the tradition of the North American deli – where the spirit of Jewish newcomers (the food of our forefathers as they settled in the new land) implanted and endeared itself to the mainstream and I believe those foods should not be forgotten. True, some 'newish-Jewish' delis pop up every once in a while, and while the menus read like a fine French menu, its real elegance spins on the familiar homey foods from the delis of yore. A lot of the time the best way to enjoy this sort of food is to make it yourself (since delis have become as rare as unicorns) so I've included all those recipes in this book, from Montreal Smoked Meat and New York Bagels to Kasha and Bowties. If I've done anything unique (in addition to adding my Jewish creations), it's that I've streamlined the recipes and perhaps made some of them a bit lighter while keeping their food soul, their culinary DNA, so to speak.

Making Jewish Food Look and Taste Great

I've always thought that great Jewish food should look and taste great. One shouldn't make jokes about hard matzoh balls or cardiac-arrest horseradish or leaden meatballs. And no more old-school, Borsht belt jokes about the evils of deli meats and chicken schmaltz. No matter how simple the dish, Jewish food tastes ambrosial whether it is kasha (kasha, aka buckwheat groats is now an 'ancient' grain' or a 'good carb' and as perfectly on trend) and bowtie pasta, Friday Night Roast Chicken or a new-spun tabbouleh and sumac.

In this cookbook, I've striven to combine the ultimate of what's classic and familiar along with newer flavours, bold incarnations and vibrant approaches. I've also included a few vegetarian recipes while once upon a time, Jewish food was 'meat and potatoes' and now it is meat, potatoes, grains, alternate proteins and innovations with vegetables and so much more! A main dish is no less hearty if it meatless and some of us have opted alternate eating pathways – so why not have some familiar Jewish food flavours in a vegetarian rendition? Plus, mixing and matching this way will ensure anyone within your family and friends circle can partake and feel welcome.

I'm proud to say that each recipe is meticulously tested by my amazing testing team and written to be accessible, low-rent in labor and yet guarantee you unmitigated success. Just like that perfect black dress with those beautiful pearls grandma gave you, you can similarly rely on these recipes knowing each will serve you well, make you look your best, and shine with a special heritage glow no matter what holiday it is or what part of your daily menu. Whether you're a great grandmother or a 30-something in your first, new household or just embarking on life with kids, these are the foods we can connect with, and share with newcomers to our family and friend fold, Jewish or not. These are recipes meant to feed body and soul. It's all caring food, created with history, significance and profound, satisfying flavours.

Where to find certain unique ingredients

Living here in Montreal can spoil you since food-wise (ditto for New Yorkers and Los Angeles cooks), there's every source of supply in terms of quality and variety. Through my recipe testers I learned that's not the case everywhere. Happily, there's the Internet, especially Amazon, because whatever my testers didn't find in their local stores (but do check out your international stores in your own city before online ordering), they did easily (and inexpensively) find online. It's not a whole lot of exotic ingredients but things like sumac (spice) and freekeh (a grain) were available online when not found in a retail store. There are online stores that specialize in spices and/or imported ingredients and sleuthing them out is a fun endeavor in and of itself.

General Notes on Ingredients

When I call for brown sugar in my recipes, I mean to imply 'light brown sugar'. Unless otherwise stated (in an instance I actually call for dark brown sugar), use light or golden variety of brown sugar.

When using oil, I generally use light olive oil. But you can also choose oil that you prefer, such as a non-GMO vegetable oil. When I specify something else (extra virgin olive oil, for example) in a recipe, I have notated it.

When it comes to spices and herbs, I use a variety of both in my recipes. I will often use both garlic powder and real garlic. One thing I rarely use (if ever) is dried parsley but I do use dried basil or oregano for example, as well as fresh.

Find a great spice store (speaking of spices) where the spices are fresh and replenished (by virtue of turnover) often. Newish Jewish cuisine, as all great cuisine, relies on vibrant, lively spices, pungent black pepper and of course kosher salt.

Kosher salt is my preference because of its purity of taste. I even prefer it to sea salt, but sea salt is also fine. Kosher salt is iodine free and totally natural and a little less salty. There are a few brands available and if it's hard to find, once you find it, stock up!

Good luck on your Jewish food experience – remember to cook with a generous heart, forget fancy, plan on quantity and simplicity and always be ready to open up your table. That said, Passover for two or Passover for forty are both equally beautiful, honorable ways to celebrate.

A few words about Kosher or mindfulness in the kitchen

The kosher laws or Kashrut whether one adheres to it or not, is probably the biggest cornerstone of Jewish cuisine. The comprehensive and detailed laws date all the way back to Moses at Mount Sinai.

When foods are prepared in accordance with the laws of kashrut, they are said to be kosher, or simply translated, "fit" or "proper". The Torah or Jewish bible does not really go much beyond presenting the laws of kashrut as a divine command guiding Jews towards holiness. However, generations of rabbis and Jewish scholars offered a rationale for kashrut based on a dual foundation of ethics and spirituality. Detailed and in-depth, the council offers cautions on both what and how we eat, found in these ancient laws, governing us on levels that transcend the mere function of eating. Some scholars postulate that the laws of Kashrut were designed this way for a purpose. For if one is always conscious and aware of what and how one eats and how this relates to other levels of daily Jewish being, our association to our faith remains strong. If the longevity of the Jews is anything to go by, this theory makes a lot of sense. In any case, the observation of kashrut has contributed its unique imprint on the development Jewish cuisine.

In the Laws of Kashrut, there are several basic tenets. First, certain foods such as shellfish and pork are forbidden. Secondly, there are specific laws on how to slaughter animals permitted for consumption. The emphasis is always on being merciful, and to avoid at all costs, any undue pain or cruelty to the animal.

In the observant Jewish kitchen, food is divided into three groups: meat, dairy, and parve foods (i.e. parve meaning foods that are neither meat nor dairy). Meat and dairy dishes are served separately from each other; parve foods can go with meat, dairy or other neutral foods including eggs, fish, fruits, tofu, nuts, grains, sugar, coffee, tea, spices, oils and vegetables.

Processed foods that are certified kosher, have been prepared under rabbinical supervision to ensure that the meat and dairy products are not mixed and that all ingredients come from sources that are certifiably kosher. Kosher certification by a reliable kashrut supervising organization is indicated by a symbol on the package.

The take-away for me, as a Jewish chef (and individual) is certainly an awareness of my own culture but more so, a distinct and beautiful mindfulness and grace about food. That's my take-away. The second part is my acknowledgement that kashrut is part and parcel to how the original Jewish recipes were created. The more you know, the more interesting things are and the more respect one has.

While adherence and interpretation of kosher laws varies, traditional or daily food, especially holiday recipes are based on this initial criterion-cum-premise. This unique code, meant to instil respect and mindfulness in food preparation and every bite you take, has also long been a strong impetus of creativity and ingenuity. Jewish cooks in Athens or Jewish cooks in Rome or Chicago might approach a matzoh ball in a few different ways but the notion of a flour-free dumpling, in a batch of Passover chicken soup is a constant. It's become such a constant, so indelible and automatic that sometimes we just do it, and pass it on, without even remembering what the original recipe was all about. How's that for endurance? It's not just good food, it's good food with roots that go way deep. That's because a huge portion of Jewish cuisine originates in the specific, symbolic dishes that correspond to the Jewish holidays. These holidays are based on either historical events (such as the Jewish exodus from Egypt, Passover) or celebrate the seasonal, agricultural calendar, (such as Sukkot), emphasizing an important bond between a people, the land and nature. Some holidays have dual roots (such as Shavuot) in both the historical and agricultural or seasonal. Jewish food is unique in that it can almost be anything as long (at least at this point in time) obeys the laws of kashrut and also, where it's appropriate, has some tethers to holidays, be it the weekly one of Shabbat or major ones such as Hanukkah and Sukkot.

All in all, it's an impressive culinary infrastructure that ensures most of whatever you eat in the Jewish kitchen has an extra layer of meaning going on. Those sentiments are pivotal things; it's a value system in fact and one that seems to stay intact because whereas things are always evolving if not totally disrupted, having a sense of grounding and having at the table, in our food, is no small nor insignificant thing. Tradition mixed with diversity, adaptation, and modifications are the hall-marks traits of Jewish culture in the kitchen as well as outside it.

On a personal note, my own food roots

To be candid, growing up, I didn't have a traditional (Jewish or otherwise) upbringing. Ours was a chaotic house, without rules, schedules, and one that didn't feature a consistent or neatly stocked pantry or fridge, so food and traditional meals times were more often catch as catch can. I suppose in part I became a chef to remedy that and/or what it bred in emotional terms. Moreover, despite a surname of Goldman (what is more classically Jewish?) *and* living but ten feet away from a synagogue I never attended, my mother (primarily) ours was a home, largely fashioned by my mother's unique values, a home that was exotic and interesting albeit often scary, lonely, disjointed. Food at home was all over the map and it seemed to me to stem from my mother's disinterest in things traditional or typical but she had an avid interest in global cuisine of her many trips, and the various housekeepers that lived with us who, happily, shared their cuisine with us. But if I learned anything about Jewish cuisine or Jewish holidays, it was at the behest of my aunt Helen who invited the extended family to her table for Passover and Rosh Hashanah. Bless Aunt Helen. Also bless Grandma Goldman who could make a delicate potato kugel that would make you weep. And bless Grandma Goldman for never, *ever* being an example of the Jewish matron who suffocated anyone with food. Annie Goldman cooked and baked with a fine hand and served generously but also elegantly. Later on, marriage brought me a mother-in-law who taught me some of the rest of what is traditional east European Jewish food. From the trio of Jewish women (my aunt, my paternal grandmother and my mother-in-law) I learned the basics of Jewish food and from my mother I inherited a good palate and also enjoyed full freedom in the kitchen so I experimented to my heart's content. Then I went and became a professional chef (pastry chef actually) and embraced the foodie movement when it began way back before the Internet. Once I became a mother of three sons, I created a Jewish table so to speak which was later expressed as my first cookbook *A Treasury of Jewish Holiday Baking*. With the background I had it might seem strange to have had a Jewish baking book as my first cookbook effort. It wasn't that I became more observant, it was because I remembered that uncomfortable sense of not having strong roots and being on the periphery. That's one thing if you *know* who you are and can make mindful choices to include or divest, but quite another if you don't really have a foundation. Food has been a huge foundation for me and in particular, Jewish food.

I tell you about my own background to remind you if you're reading this book and however Jewish or not Jewish you are or however atypical or even orphaned (or not) you might feel with your heritage (culturally speaking or simply via your own family narrative), I welcome you to *my* table. This is *our* book - all of us! It is Jewish heritage food to be sure but I hope you feel the embracive-ness and inclusion which is my intent. So, welcome to my table. I hope you enjoy this cookbook. Share the food and the recipes. Remember to gather, to celebrate, to appreciate and to eat well.

Chapter One
Brunch and Breakfast

Come for Breakfast, Stay for Brunch!

I grew up with a father who made breakfast on the week days or weekend an awesome affair. He paid meticulous attention to each detail: the coffee was hot and deeply brewed, the toast was buttered just so, and the poached eggs done to a turn. Those memories and the appetite for those foods have stayed with me ever since, and I'm not surprised the first meal of the day is my favorite meal of the day. But seriously, who doesn't love an invite for breakfast or brunch? What's really nice about an invite for breakfast or brunch? What's really appealing about this starter meal is that breakfast or brunch is customarily (and happily) casual but at the same time, it's always hearty, nutritious and vibrant with comforting, basic tastes of cheese, orange juice, eggs and rustic breads (rye toast or bagels). Since morning is my best time of day, along with the typical morning foods, brunch/breakfast is already starting in the best of places in my books.

The Tradition of the "Jewish Brunch" since the 1930s

In North America, brunch seems to have been invented around the 1930s. In 1939, the *New York Times*, who should know, described Sunday as a two-meal day – we can presume that meant brunch and then a light supper. In the '60s, brunch was so popular there were whole cookbooks devoted to it and by the '90s, boomers armed with little kids and the happy grandparents unofficially made Saturday another official brunch day. Incidentally, 'breakfast out' or breakfast at a friend's house constitutes: brunch. Why do we think as brunch as a 'Jewish' thing? Well, demographically, the incidences of brunch (via restaurant and population data) show a preponderance of brunch participation in states wherein the Jewish population is also stronger. Some suggest the Sunday brunch was something to do when one's neighbors were off at church services; others suggest that the neighborhood deli, always a great place to meet, was ideal for a more relaxing Sunday gathering when presumably, many people weren't at work. Deli-style breakfast food came from breakfast foods at home and vice versa and brunch out, or brunch in, is always a positive and popular thing! Last, the dairy component of the Jewish diet, part of the old laws of Kashrut, also suggest a hankering for all things dairy as a result. In other words, it was part of being kosher and segued to a simple love of dairy or parve foods. Chicken soup and matzoh balls is one person's comfort food, but bagels and cream cheese or warm cheese blintzes can make someone else beam with gratitude.

What is it about a Jewish Brunch?

So what is it about the Jewish tradition of brunch? For one thing, it's easy: if you have bagels, cream cheese and some coffee, you have brunch. Call up some people, pull out chairs, toast those bagels, sit back and talk and you have a feast. It's also low tech, low cost (a couple dozen fresh bagels go a long way) and suits everyone's diet of the moment. Brunch turns an ordinary moment in the early part of any given day into an event. Not appended to any particular holiday on the Jewish calendar, brunch easily takes on the feel of a celebration. There's just something about breakfast and brunch that is part of the Jewish cultural culinary code. Business start-ups or legacy office affairs can be done over a bagel breakfast or deli-style mish-mash (an omelet with salami, peppers and onions).

No matter how modest, brunch is a made-in-the-shade success. If you add other things: more spreads, cold salads (hummus, eggplant, Shatchouka), a little lox, a quiche or two, and a babka? Oh my goodness! You've made a memorable occasion. Brunch also is one of those things you can have ready in under an hour and the guest list can be but one other person or swell to a dozen and it is still easy to do.

Herein is a veritable spread, as it were, of my best brunch and breakfast favorite recipes, Jewish-style. You'll also find some extra ideas in the Salad and Appetizer chapters. It's also good to know that in general, whatever works as a brunch offering is usually just as welcome at Shavuot, Yom Kippur (before and after) or a vegetarian Saturday night supper.

So, what are you waiting for? Come for brunch!

Old-Fashioned Cheese Blintzes

These thin Jewish-style crepes are made with pantry-available ingredients and are so satisfying with their traditional cheese filling. This dish is perfect for Sunday brunch, a festive Shavuot or Hanukkah buffet.

*Dry cottage cheese is also known as hoop or baker's cheese or no-curd dry cottage cheese or farmer's cheese.

For the Blintz Batter, place the flour, salt, and sugar in a food processor and blend briefly. Add the seltzer or milk, eggs, butter and vanilla and whiz to blend into a thin batter, about 15 seconds. Let batter rest 15 minutes. Meanwhile, make the filling.

For the Cheese Filling, in a medium bowl, using a fork or spoon, blend the farmer's cheese or cottage cheese with the egg yolk, sugar, lemon juice and sour cream.

To fill Blintzes, fill each crepe with 2-3 tablespoons of filling on the lower third of the browned side of the blintz, fold two sides inwards, and then roll up into bundles.

To fry the Blintzes, heat pan to medium hot and dab in some butter or oil. Spoon on about 2-4 tablespoons of batter, depending on size of crepes desired (use only enough to coat pan) and tilt pan to spread the batter all around. Cook until bottom browns. Turn over and cook for 2-3 more minutes. Keep blintzes warm (cover with foil on a plate) until all of batter is used up. Serve with sour cream, Greek yogurt, or fresh fruit.

Makes about 12-16

Blintzes

1 cup all-purpose flour

1/8 teaspoon salt

1 tablespoon sugar

1½ cups seltzer water or warm milk or seltzer water

2 eggs

2 tablespoons unsalted butter or margarine, melted

1 teaspoon pure vanilla extract, optional

Cheese Filling

1 pound farmer's or dry cottage cheese *

1 egg yolk

2½ tablespoons sugar

2 teaspoons fresh lemon juice

4 tablespoons sour cream

Butter or oil

Blintz Soufflé Casserole

Great for a brunch or any time, this is a great holiday or long weekend dish. Nothing beats a make-head dish especially when it puffs up so impressively. Use prepared blintzes or make your own with the recipe here. A perfect dish to serve to out-of-towners who've come in for a bar mitzvah or as a pre-Yom Kippur main dairy dish.

Blintz Batter

½ teaspoon salt

¾ cup flour

1 1/3 cup milk

2 tablespoons oil or melted butter

Filling

1 pound cottage cheese, dry type *

2 eggs

2 tablespoons sugar

¼ teaspoon salt

1 tablespoon flour

Topping

¼ cup unsalted butter, melted

¼ cup sugar

¼ teaspoon salt

2 cups sour cream or Greek yogurt

6 eggs

2 teaspoons pure vanilla extract

* Also known

as no-curd, hoop or "baker's" cheese

For the blintzes, combine everything in a food processor, blender or bowl, to make a smooth batter. Let batter rest 15 minutes. Heat a 9-inch crepe pan or non-stick skillet and dab in some butter. Smear on about ¼ cup of crepe batter to coat the pan. Cook until bottom browns and then turn over once to cook other side until it too is nicely browned. Stack the crepes with a sheet of parchment paper between each one to prevent sticking. Finish making crepes warm until all of batter is used up. You should have 12-18 blintzes.

For the filling, in a food processor, blend the cottage cheese, eggs, sugar, salt and flour to a smooth texture. Fill each blintz by placing a heaping tablespoonful of filling onto one side of the crepe or blintz. Fold in one side and roll in remaining ends. Use a dot or two of butter in a non-stick frypan to fry the blintzes, browning blintzes a few at a time on each side until lightly browned.

Preheat oven to 350°. Spray a 9 by 13 inch pan with non-stick cooking spray and line pan with the blintzes. For the Topping, in a medium bowl, blend the butter, sugar, sour cream, eggs, vanilla and salt. Pour topping over the blintzes. Bake one hour or until the casserole is slightly Serve warm with fresh berries.

6-8 servings

Shakshuka with Poached Eggs

This is also known as Salade Cuite or in other parts of the Middle East (certainly Israel) as Shakshuka. It's a North African red pepper, tomato ratatouille or 'stew' that's the quintessential pita mop. There are countless variations of this dish and many ways to serve it but I love it as a stylish breakfast dish, with poached eggs atop the beautiful base of tomatoes and spice. This recipe makes enough for the dish and leftovers to keep as a dipping or side 'salad' (for pita wedges, for example) If you have some zhoug on hand, a Yemenite green chili dish, that would be added zest.

In very 12-14 inch skillet, heat olive oil over medium heat. Add red peppers and cook, lowering heat and stirring to soften, 10-15 minutes. Add in onions and garlic and cook 5 minutes more just to soften onions and garlic. Preheat oven to 325°.

To the pan, add canned tomatoes, salt, pepper, chili flakes, cumin, coriander, paprika and lemon juice. Simmer on the stove on very low heat for 30-45 minutes, stirring every so often until mixture thickens and smells very fragrant. Season to taste. Keep half to use in the poached egg dish and refrigerate the other half to serve as a side salad or dip.

Preparing Poached Eggs and Shakshuka

Place half the batch of Shatchouka in a 10-12 inch deep skillet and warm on low. Into each quadrant of the pan, break open an egg. Cover the pan to allow poached egg to set, 10-12 minutes. Serve egg with some sauce for each portion and dust with cilantro and parsley.

Makes 4-5 cups, approximately

¼ cup olive oil

3 medium red peppers, coarsely diced

1 medium onion, diced fine

1 tablespoon minced garlic

1 28 ounce can ground tomatoes

½ teaspoon salt

¼ teaspoon pepper

¼ teaspoon dry chili flakes

2 teaspoons cumin

1½ teaspoon coriander

1 tablespoon paprika

1 tablespoon fresh lemon juice

1-2 tablespoons zhoug, optional

Finishing Touches

Eggs, for poaching
Cilantro, parsley, finely minced

Poached Eggs on Latkes with Avocado and Hollandaise

Poached eggs are a classic, avocado is trendy; serving both on a homey latke (instead of English Muffins) is inspired! This is designed to impress and coincidentally delicious!

Avocado Part

4 ripe avocados,
peeled and pitted

¼ cup lime juice

1 small red onion, diced

2 tablespoons chopped cilantro

½ teaspoon garlic powder

Potato Pancakes or Latkes

4 medium potatoes, peeled

3 eggs

2 tablespoons flour
(or matzoh meal)

2 teaspoons kosher salt

3/8 teaspoon black pepper

6 tablespoons light olive oil

Poached Eggs

8 eggs

2 tablespoons vinegar

Salt, pepper

In a medium bowl, combine the avocado with lime juice and salt. Mix and mash with the back of a fork until slightly chunky. Add onions, cilantro, and garlic powder and mix to combine. Cover with plastic wrap and press down so the wrap is touching the top of the guacamole directly. Set aside.

For the potato pancakes, shred or grate potatoes using a food processor or box grater. Place potatoes in a bowl and add the eggs, flour, salt and pepper and mix well. Add olive oil to the hot pan. Form potato batter into ¼ cup patties, about ½ inch thick and gently place in hot oil. Fry 3-5 minutes per side or until golden brown and crispy. Drain on paper towels and repeat with remaining batter. Keep warm on a plate under tented foil.

To poach eggs, fill a large saucepan with at least 2 inches of water and add the vinegar. Let water come to a simmer and stir. Crack one egg at a time in the center of the circle, cooking only cooking about 4 eggs at a time; cook for 3-4 minutes. Remove eggs with a slotted spoon to drain and place on a plate until ready for assembly. Repeat with remaining eggs.

To serve, top each potato pancake with 3 tablespoons of the avocado mixture and a poached egg. Season with salt and pepper.

6-8 servings

Cheesecake-Stuffed French Toast with Cidered Apples

What's better than a mash-up of two favorites from the Jewish kitchen, cheesecake and challah? This is a superb company dish that you can prepare the night before. The caramelized braised apples draw raves at brunch or holidays that have dairy dishes as a food symbols.

Cheesecake Filling

1 8 ounce package cream cheese softened

1/3 cup sugar

2 eggs

2 teaspoons pure vanilla extract

¼ cup flour

8 thick slices challah, cut 2½ inch thick

For the Cheesecake Filling, in a mixer bowl, blend the cream cheese, sugar, eggs, vanilla, and flour together and set aside.

Make a cut deeply into each slice of the thick slices of challah/bread to make a pocket. Fill with 2-3 tablespoons cheesecake filling. Alternatively, you can slather cheesecake filling between two thinner slices of bread (i.e. cut a thick slice in half, diagonally, and fill with filling, and gently top with the other half).

For the Egg Bath, to a medium mixer bowl, mix the eggs, cream, flour, sugar, vanilla, baking powder and butter until smooth, 1-2 minutes. Soak each challah slice in the egg bath 5 minutes. Heat some butter in a large non-stick pan. Over medium heat sauté each piece on each side to brown evenly. Place in a casserole dish.

For the Cidered Apples, heat the butter in a medium pan. Over low heat stir in brown sugar and cider and mix well; then quickly add in apples and cook until they are softened, over low heat, about 15 minutes. Serve apples over French toast and drizzle with apple or maple syrup.

Serves 4-6

Egg Bath

6 eggs

½ cup cream or milk

¼ cup flour

3 tablespoons sugar

1 teaspoon pure vanilla extract

½ teaspoon baking powder

¼ cup unsalted butter, melted

Cidered Apple Topping

¼ cup unsalted butter

½ cup brown sugar

½ cup apple cider or juice

4 cups diced, peeled apples

Finishing Touches

Butter

Maple syrup

Montreal Cheese Bagels

If you're a Montrealer, ex-pat or have a Montreal foodie relative, you know exactly why this recipe is gold. Imagine a blintz filling tucked inside a buttery puff dough roll and then topped with sour cream. This is the most requested food to tote to state-side friends and family. Use the easy pastry recipe here or swap with store-bought puff dough.

Quick Puff Pastry

2 cups all-purpose flour

¼ teaspoon salt

2 teaspoons baking powder

1 tablespoon sugar

½ cup unsalted butter, cut into chunks

½ cup sour cream

1 egg

Filling

1 pound dry cottage cheese *

1 egg

1/3 cup sugar

1/8 teaspoon salt

2 teaspoons fresh lemon juice

Finishing Touches

2 tablespoons flour

Egg wash, sugar

* Dry cottage cheese is also known as hoop or baker's cheese or no-curd dry cottage cheese

For the Quick Puff Pastry, place flour, salt, baking powder and sugar in food processor. Pulse to blend. Add butter chunks and pulse to cut fat into flour. Add in the sour cream and egg and process to form a soft dough. Wrap dough and chill about 20 minutes.

For the Filling, in a mixer or food processor, blend the cottage cheese, egg, sugar, salt, lemon juice and flour to make a smooth, thick filling. Chill for ten minutes. Preheat oven to 350°.

To form the cheese bagels, divide dough in half. Roll out on a lightly floured board to an oblong ¼ inch thick. Place half of filling along one edge. Roll half way then cut the roll you have formed away from the remaining body of the dough. Repeat so you have two oblongs.

Cut into 8-inch lengths and place on a parchment lined baking sheet. Curve each roll into horse shoe shapes, pinching ends together to seal. Brush with beaten egg and sprinkle lightly with sugar. Bake about 40 minutes or until lightly browned.

Makes 12

Mish-Mash or Jewish Deli Style Western Omelet

Mention the term 'mish-mash' outside a deli, and people may assume you've borrowed your toddler's vocabulary. Mish-Mash actually refers to a modified Western omelet and it's a Sunday brunch deli staple. This recipe may be increased as needed.

In a medium sized skillet, heat the olive oil or margarine over medium heat. Stir in the onions and green peppers and cook to soften (2-3 minutes). Add the salami and cook 2 minutes to brown slightly. Whip the eggs with the cold water and add to vegetable mixture in pan. Cook over medium heat, pulling cooked sections of the omelets into center, allowing raw egg batter to run out to sides until mixture is evenly cooked. Add salt and pepper lightly.

Serve immediately.

Serves 1-2

2 tablespoons light olive oil or unsalted margarine
¼ cup chopped onions
¼ cup chopped green pepper
1/3 cup chopped all-beef salami
4 eggs
2 tablespoons cold water
Salt, pepper

Romanian Cottage Cheese Cornmeal Kugel

Also known as malai, *this is a superb dish for at Yom Kippur Yom Kippur or because it's cheese-based, it's ideal with Shavuot or Hanukkah or as a brunch offering. It's wonderful warm from the oven topped with cherry topping and/or sour cream or Greek yogurt.*

Batter

1/3 cup melted unsalted butter or oil

1/3 cup sugar

2 eggs

¼ cup milk

1/3 cup sour cream or yogurt

1 cup all-purpose flour

1 cup cornmeal

2 teaspoons baking powder

1/8 teaspoon salt

Cheese Filling

1 pound dry cottage cheese *

1/3 cup sugar

1 teaspoon pure vanilla extract

2 eggs

½ cup sour cream or yogurt

1/8 teaspoon salt

Finishing Touches

Sour cream or Greek yogurt
Fresh berries

* Dry cottage cheese is also known as hoop or baker's cheese or no-curd dry cottage cheese

Preheat oven to 350°. Grease an 11 by 7 inch rectangular dish. You can also make this dish in a 9 or 10-inch spring form pan.

For the batter, in a medium bowl, whisk the butter, sugar, eggs, milk, sour cream or yogurt, flour, cornmeal, baking powder and salt until smooth. For cheese filling, in a food processor, blend the cottage cheese with the sugar, vanilla, eggs, sour cream or yogurt and salt.

Spoon half of cornmeal batter into dish. Top with half of cheese filling, and then finish with more cornmeal batter and cheese batter. Marbleize the mixture by gently swirling a butter knife through mixture.

Bake until casserole appears set, about 40-50 minutes. Serve warm or chilled, with sour cream or yogurt and berries.

8-10 servings

Smoked Salmon and Dill Cream Cheese Brunch Pizza

One of the easiest, most extravagant, restaurant-looking recipes you'll ever make. This is perfect for lunch, brunch, or early supper, combining two of the best flavours of Jewish cuisine: lox and cream cheese. Store-bought pizza dough is also a good time-saver here but the recipe is easy!

For the Pizza Dough, in a mixer bowl, blend the water, yeast, half of the flour, salt, and olive oil, adding in additional flour as required to make soft dough. Knead eight minutes until smooth. Cover dough and let rise 45-60 minutes. Gently deflate and let rise until needed (anywhere from one to three hours) on the counter. If you're using it the next day, wrap it up and refrigerate.

To make pizza, divide dough in three. Line three baking sheets with parchment paper and drizzle on some olive oil. Flatten each portion of dough to make a 9-inch pizza and place on the prepared baking sheet. Preheat oven to 450°.

Top each pizza with some olive oil, salt, pepper and garlic. Spread cream cheese and feta cheese (in dollops). Top with onion, olives, tomatoes, dill and disperse lox last. Brush the pizza crust edges with olive oil and sprinkle on sesame seeds. Bake until top is bubbling and rim is coloured, 7-12 minutes.

Three 9-inch pizzas

Pizza Dough

½ teaspoon instant yeast

1½ cups water

4-5 cups all-purpose flour

1¾ teaspoon salt

1 teaspoon sugar

2 tablespoons olive oil

Topping

2 teaspoons olive oil

Salt, pepper

1 small clove garlic, finely minced

4 tablespoons cream cheese

1/3 cup feta cheese, crumbled

1 small red onion, thinly sliced

¼ cup black olives, sliced

2 plum tomatoes, sliced

1 tablespoon fresh minced dill

2 ounces minced smoked lox

Sesame seeds

Sweet Cheese Corn Flaked-Topped Dairy Kugel

A very appealing brunch dish, this is perfect for break-the-fast on Yom Kippur or as a dairy main dish for Shavuot or a Shabbat luncheon. The recipe doubles well and can be offered with sour cream or fresh fruit. Comfort food at its finest hour!

1 12-ounce packages egg noodles cooked according to package directions

1/3 cup melted unsalted butter or oil

6 eggs

1 cup sour cream

2 cups small curd cottage cheese

½ cup whipping cream

2 teaspoons pure vanilla extract

½ cup sugar

1/8 teaspoon salt

Corn Flake Streusel Topping

2 cups crushed corn flake cereal

¼ cup unsalted butter, melted

½ teaspoon pure vanilla extract

1 teaspoon cinnamon

Pinch nutmeg

1 tablespoon sugar

Prepare the noodles according the package directions; drain and place in a large bowl. Spray a 9 by 13 inch pan with non-stick cooking spray and place on a baking sheet lined with parchment paper. Preheat oven to 350°

Cool the noodles to room temperature and add in the butter, eggs, sour cream, cottage cheese, whipping cream, vanilla, sugar and salt. Spoon into prepared pan.

For the Corn Flake Streusel Topping, place the corn flakes, butter, vanilla, cinnamon, nutmeg and sugar in a bowl and mix together. Sprinkle the streusel over top of noodles.

Bake until top is lightly browned, 30-45 minutes.

Serves 8-10

Nova Bagel Schmear

A little lox, aka smoked salmon, blended into cream cheese makes the ultimate lox schmear. Bring this out at your next brunch, a dairy-based holiday occasion, a baby shower, breakfast for the 'out-of-towners' attending a bar mitzvah, wedding, a bris or just as a bagel snack!

In a medium bowl, using a spatula, gently blend the cream cheese with the onions. When softened, add in the pepper, salt, lox and dill; blend gently to combine. Keep refrigerated until serving time.

Makes 1 cup

8 ounces cream cheese softened

¼ cup red onions or chives, coarsely minced

¼ teaspoon black pepper

1/8 teaspoon salt

½ cup minced lox or smoked salmon

1 teaspoon minced fresh dill

Cinnamon Honey Cream Cheese Bagel Schmear

Bagels are as easily matched up with toppings sweet as well as the savoury; after Lox Schmear, nothing is as appealing as cinnamon-scented cream cheese spread on fresh bagels. Serve this with other spreads to make a bagel buffet.

8 ounces cream cheese, softened

1 tablespoon honey

2-3 teaspoons cinnamon

½ cup raisins, optional

In a medium bowl, using a spatula, gently blend the cream cheese with the honey and then with a fork, blend in the cinnamon. Don't blend the cinnamon so that it's totally homogenous; some streaking or uneven white and cinnamon-tinted cream cheese is more appealing. Keep refrigerated until serving time.

Makes 1 cup

Coffee Cake Muffins

Coffee cake is always welcome, especially at brunch. This mini version, aka muffins, is perfect for break-the-fast gatherings and anytime you prefer not to make a big coffeecake.

Preheat oven to 350°. Line a large baking sheet with parchment paper. Arrange the oven rack to the upper third or middle of the oven.

Line a baking sheet with parchment paper. Spray a muffin tin very generously with non-stick cooking spray. Line nine muffin cups with muffin liners. Place on baking sheet.

Prepare the streusel by pulsing the butter, flour, brown sugar, white sugar, cinnamon and walnuts together a few minutes or less to get a crumbly mixture. Set aside.

For the muffins, in a large mixer bowl, hand whisk the brown sugar with the oil and butter. Whisk in the eggs, vanilla and buttermilk well. Fold in the flour, salt, baking powder, and baking soda to make a smooth batter. Fold in the apples and blend well. Using a large muffin scooper, scoop huge gobs of batter into muffin cups to three-quarters full. Top each with an equal amount of the streusel topping.

Bake at 20 minutes; turn muffins around and bake another 15-22 minutes until done, lowering temperature to 350° if they are browning too fast. Let stand 15 minutes before attempting to remove muffins from pan (let them set up and get more solid).

Makes 9 large muffins

Vanilla Cinnamon Streusel Topping

¼ cup unsalted butter

3 tablespoons flour

1/3 cup brown sugar

2 tablespoons white sugar

½ teaspoon cinnamon

1/3 cup finely chopped walnuts

Batter

1½ cups golden brown sugar, firmly packed

½ cup unsalted butter, melted

¼ cup vegetable oil

2 teaspoons pure vanilla extract

2 eggs

1 cup buttermilk

3 cups all-purpose flour

3/8 teaspoon salt

2½ teaspoons baking powder

½ teaspoon baking soda

3 cups peeled, diced apples, optional

Quiche-in-a-Loaf

This outstanding and time-saving but elegant brunch dish that's as good warm or chilled. Serve it as a main dish with salad or in small squares as a finger food appetizer. Make this ahead or whip it up an hour before serving. It's both simple and elegant.

1 cup all-purpose flour

1 teaspoon baking powder

2 teaspoons salt

¼ teaspoon pepper

1 teaspoon garlic powder

2 tablespoons minced fresh parsley

1 cup water or vegetable stock

1/3 cup light olive oil

3 tablespoons white wine

½ cup light cream

6 eggs

½ cup minced scallions

½ cup minced black or green olives

½ cup minced sun-dried tomatoes or roasted red peppers

2 cups shredded white cheddar cheese

1 cup shredded Swiss or mozzarella

Finishing Touches

2 tablespoons grated Parmesan

Paprika

Preheat oven to 350°. Spray two 8 by 4 inch or one angel food cake pan (s) with non-stick cooking spray.

In a food processor, add the flour, baking powder, salt, pepper, garlic powder and parsley and blend one minute. Add in the water or vegetable bouillon, oil, wine, light cream, and eggs. Fold in scallions, olives, sun dried tomatoes or roasted red pepper and cheeses and blend to a smooth batter 1-2 minutes. Spoon into pan and dust top with Parmesan cheese and paprika.

Bake until set, 45-55 minutes. Quiche is done when the top surface springs back when lightly touched and is browned around edges. Cool 10-15 minutes before serving. If you're not serving immediately, refrigerate. Serve in cut in half-inch slices with a side salad, salsa in two-inch squares as an appetizer.

Serves 8-12, depending on portion size

Vanilla Cinnamon Challah Bread Pudding

What's more ambrosial than chunks of challah bread pulled together in a creamy batter of eggs, evaporated milk and vanilla-studded with tender morsels of apples and kissed with a hint of cinnamon. French toast is where leftover challah usually ends up, but this bread pudding is right on trend. This is especially welcome as a Jewish New Year holiday side dish, Yom Kippur, Shavuot or of course, brunch!

Preheat oven to 350°. Lightly spray a 9 by 13 inch baking dish with non-stick cooking spray. Place it on a parchment paper lined baking sheet.

Melt butter and cool. Prepare apples and set aside. Prepare challah chunks by cutting into cubes.

Place the bread cubes in a large mixer bowl. In another bowl, mix together the evaporated milk, milk, light cream, eggs, sugar, butter, vanilla, cinnamon, baking powder and salt. Pour over bread cubes and let stand 10 minutes to absorb. Fold in apples and raisins. Spoon into prepared pan; dust the top with a little confectioner's sugar and cinnamon.

Bake until set, about 35-40 minutes. Serve warm or cold.

Serves 8-10

2 cups coarsely chopped, peeled apples

10 cups leftover challah cubes

1½ cups evaporated milk

1 cup milk

1 cup light cream

8 eggs

1 cup sugar

½ cup unsalted butter melted

2 teaspoons pure vanilla extract

1 teaspoon cinnamon

2 teaspoons baking powder

1/8 teaspoon salt

½ cup raisins, optional

Finishing Touches

Confectioners' sugar

Cinnamon

Gooey Cinnamon Babka

This recipe is not only easy, but it makes a just-right sized babka, perfect for a weekend's munching or a coffee klatch with friends. It's better-than-any-bakery and features layer after layer of sweet, cinnamon, rippling throughout a butter and vanilla sweet dough.

Sweet Dough

¼ cup water

2½ teaspoons instant yeast

5 cups all-purpose flour

½ cup warm milk

3 eggs

2½ teaspoons pure vanilla extract

½ cup sugar

½ teaspoon salt

¾ cup unsalted butter softened, in chunks

Cinnamon Filling

1½ cup brown sugar, firmly packed

1/3 cup all-purpose flour

4 tablespoons unsalted butter melted

1 cup miniature marshmallows *

4 teaspoons cinnamon

Butter Crumb Topping

4 tablespoons unsalted butter softened

½ cup confectioners' sugar

½ cup all-purpose flour

Finishing Touches

Egg wash

*Marshmallows make for a quick and gooey cinnamon filling. If you don't have some on hand, use two egg whites and two tablespoons sugar whipped together until glossy.

For the Sweet Dough, in a mixer bowl of a mixer, whisk together water and yeast. Briskly stir in one cup of the flour, then the warm milk, the eggs, vanilla, sugar, salt, butter and most of the remaining flour, holding back a cup until you see what is required. Mix the dough and then, with dough hook, knead on slow speed 8-10 minutes, until smooth and elastic and is a soft (versus bouncy) dough. Remove the dough hook from the mixer, spray the dough with non-stick cooking spray and cover the entire mixer (bowl, machine and all) with a large plastic bag. Allow to rise until puffy, about 45-90 minutes.

For the Cinnamon Filling, in a bowl or a food processor, blend the sugar, flour, butter, marshmallows and cinnamon to make a thick (and uneven) filling.

For the Butter Crumb Topping, in a small bowl, with your fingertips, rub or cut butter, confectioners' sugar and flour together to make a crumbly topping. Set aside.

When the dough has risen, gently press down and turn onto a lightly floured board. Pat dough into a 12 by 20 inch rectangle. Let rest while preparing baking pan.

Line a baking sheet with parchment paper. Generously spray a 12-inch angel food cake pan with pan with non-stick cooking spray. Line edges and bottom with cut-out pieces of parchment paper; place pan on baking sheet.

Pat two-thirds of the Cinnamon Filling all over dough surface, pressing slightly. Roll up dough into a large jellyroll and press down a little bit. Smear with remaining Cinnamon Filling. Bring two ends of the dough into the center (to meet each other) and press slightly to lock so you have a circle. Using your hands, twist the nine and three o'clock positions of the circle and twist to make a twisted oblong. Place in the prepared pan. Brush with egg wash and sprinkle top with Butter Crumb Topping. Cover the entire sheet with a large plastic bag. Let rise until babka is flush or over top of pan, 45-90 minutes.

Preheat oven to 350°. Bake 55-65 minutes or until the babka is medium brown. Cool in pan fifteen minutes before removing to a rack or serving plate.

Makes one babka

Challah Monkey Bread

Nothing is easier to put together than a simple challah dough, converted to a cinnamon-kissed Monkey Bread coffee cake. Wonderful pull-apart baking!

Dough

4 teaspoons instant yeast

1 cup warm water

3-4 cups all-purpose flour

¼ cup sugar

2 tablespoons honey

1 teaspoon salt

2 teaspoons pure vanilla extract

1/3 cup vegetable oil

2 eggs

Dipping Cinnamon Sugar

½ cup unsalted butter, melted

½ cup brown sugar

½ cup white sugar

1 tablespoon cinnamon

Glaze

1 cup confectioners' sugar

1-2 tablespoons light cream

½ teaspoon pure vanilla extract

For the dough, in a mixer bowl, whisk the yeast and water. Briskly stir in 2 cups of the flour, sugar, honey, salt, sugar, vanilla, oil and eggs. Blend well with a wood spoon and then start kneading with a dough hook and mixer on low speed. Add in additional flour as required to make a soft dough, 5-8 minutes. Place both dough in a bowl that has been sprayed with non-stick cooking spray and insert in a large plastic bag. Allow to rise until almost doubled in size, 45-60 minutes.

Preheat the oven to 350°. Spray a 12-inch angel food cake pan with non-stick cooking spray. (It's better to use a one-piece angel food cake pan, not one with a removable bottom). Line a baking sheet with parchment paper and place pan on it.

Meanwhile, for the Dipping Cinnamon Sugar, mix the butter, brown sugar, white sugar and cinnamon together. Gently deflate the dough and place on a floured surface. Pat into an 8-inch square and cut into eight strips. Cut each strip into eight squares. Roll each square into a little ball. Using a fork, dip each ball into the cinnamon sugar butter mixture. Arrange balls of dough in prepared cake pan. Insert pan into a plastic bag and let rise until almost doubled, about 45 minutes or until dough balls are within a ½ inch of the top rim of the pan.

Bake 30 minutes or until golden brown.

For the Glaze, in a medium bowl, stir together the confectioners' sugar, cream and vanilla extract. Unmold the bread on a serving plate and drizzle with the glaze.

Best served warm, leftovers are perfect for bread pudding.

Makes one large bread

New York Style Water Bagels

These sassy bagels are also known as water bagels. If the secret ingredient, as New Yorkers brag, is the water, then we out-of-towners are out of luck. Minus the Hudson River, these bagels are as authentic as famed H&H Bagels! The malt powder is optional but available from King Arthur Flour.

In a mixer bowl, whisk together water, yeast, and sugar. Let stand a couple of minutes to allow yeast to dissolve. Briskly whisk in in oil, malt and one cup of flour. Add salt, then most of remaining flour, kneading 10-12 minutes to make very stiff dough, adding in more flour if required.

Cover with a tea towel and let dough rest on a board about 15 minutes. Meanwhile, line two large baking sheets with baking parchment and sprinkle generously with corn meal. Fill a large pot two-thirds full of water; add the malt syrup and salt. Bring water to a gentle boil. Preheat oven to 450°.

Divide dough into 10 sections and form into 10-inch long strips. Roll the ends together to seal and make a ring. Place on a very lightly floured surface near your stove. Let bagels rest 15-20 minutes.

Prepare two more baking sheets - line one with a kitchen towel and the other with parchment paper which has been sprinkled with cornmeal, if desired. Reduce water to simmer and add bagels a few at a time. Allow to come to surface and simmer thirty seconds. Turn over and cook other side about 45 seconds more. Place on prepared towel-lined baking sheet. Leave plain or sprinkle with sesame or poppy seeds. Place in oven, reduce heat to 425° and bake until done, about 17-22 minutes, turning bagels once, when almost baked.

Makes 10

1½ cups warm water

1 tablespoon instant yeast

1 tablespoon sugar

1 tablespoon oil

2 teaspoons malt powder, optional

2 teaspoons salt

4½ - 5½ cups bread flour

Kettle Water

6 quarts water

2 tablespoons malt syrup or honey, optional

1 teaspoon salt

Finishing Touches

Cornmeal, optional

Sesame, poppy seeds

Chapter Two
Appetizers and Starters

Appetizers and Starters

It would be a cinch do a *whole* book on appetizers since they are such a beloved and integral part of the Jewish menu. Snacky, informal, homey or (in Yiddish) *haimish* appetizers, also known as starters or *forspeizen,* are tasty bites. On most tables even ever-popular hummus counts in as an appetizer since it often is offered before a meal. Appetizers also work as side dishes *with* a meal shebang. It's just in the planning and intention, that is, what sort of event or Jewish holiday you're hosting.

Just as it sounds, appetizers are that something to have before the meal, intended to wake up the palate and dampen the appetite just a bit, so your guests don't overdo the main meal. When we're slightly sated, big meals are more enjoyable and leisurely. Appetizers could be mini knishes or brisket sliders, or they could be an array of dishes like different flavours of hummus, salade cuit with pita wedges or squares of rye bread topped with chopped liver and onions.

Sometimes appetizers, being small and often times are hand-formed, can take some time to prepare. But in many cases (anything made with puff pastry or filo, for instance) you can make a variety of appetizers and freeze them. This way you're prepared for a bigger event such as a holiday meal or drop-by visitors of an impromptu bunch or just as a snack for your best friend who appears at your doorstep, hungry and ready to chat over something deliciously savoury and homemade.

These recipes are hand-chosen in that they are classic for the most part but vitally revamped, especially flavourful, and feature international or global Jewish spice notes as well as mash-ups.

Baked Figs, Camembert and Honey

This is a gorgeous Sukkot dish but lovely for a brunch or any dairy meal. With its biblical vibe of honey and figs offering a luscious, velvety flavor palate, nothing is more satisfying. Feel free to swap in feta or chevre cheese instead of feta.

Preheat oven to 375°.

Trim the top and side surfaces of cheese (the white 'rind') just a bit and make some score marks on the top surface. Brush with the oil and drizzle with the honey. Place the cheese in a small round ceramic baking dish that just fits the cheese. Bake 10 minutes or until cheese starts to soften.

Lower temperate to 350° and add sliced figs on top of the cheese and dust with a pinch of rosemary, salt and pepper and bake 5-10 minutes more. Serve immediately with baguette rounds.

Serves 4-5

1 6-8 inch camembert cheese wheel

1 teaspoon light olive oil

2 teaspoons honey

3-4 fresh figs, sliced

Fresh rosemary

Coarse salt, pepper

Apples, Honey and Goat Cheese Crostini

I think these are just perfect for Rosh Hashanah or anytime you want something that is salty, sweet and a touch tart. You can play around with flavors here. I also use slivered dried figs with a drizzle of balsamic vinegar syrup; you can also switch a soft goat feta for the Chevre cheese.

1 baguette sliced in ½ inch rounds

Olive oil

6 ounces Chevre cheese

2 apples such as Honey Crisp

½ cup finely chopped walnuts

Greek honey

Pomegranate arils

Fresh figs, sliced

Preheat oven to 375°. Line a large baking sheet with parchment paper. Place bread rounds on baking sheet and drizzle lightly with oil. Place in oven to brown, about 15 minutes.

Meanwhile, slice apples and have walnuts, honey, pomegranate arils and sliced figs nearby.

Spread some cheese on each bread round. Top with some apple slices, walnuts, pomegranate arils and slices of figs. Drizzle each with some honey.

Serves 6-8

Zhoug

Zhoug is kind of a spicy, green salsa that hails from Yemen and is considered Israel's Sriracha. I think of it as a green, hot and mean ketchup which enlivens pita bread wedges, scrambled eggs, a bowl of hummus or works as a great topping on Shakshuka.

Place all of the ingredients in a small food processor. Blitz in a few pulses to get a coarse paste; make sure not to overmix. Serve with pita bread wedges, fish, chicken, in sandwiches or swirled into hummus.

About 2/3 cup

½ bunch of cilantro, chopped

½ cup parsley, chopped

2 hot green chillies, chopped

½ teaspoon cumin

¼ teaspoon cardamom

¼ teaspoon cloves

1/8 teaspoon sugar

¼ teaspoon salt

1 garlic clove, minced

2 tablespoons olive oil

2 tablespoons water

Fried Dill Pickles

This really updates the deli's favorite child: dill pickles. Sliced and gently fried to a golden brown, this is a sour-salty snack that is perfect with pastrami sandwiches or on a Sukkot buffet. These are customarily served with a dipping sauce of Ranch Dressing.

6-8 large dill pickles cut in ½ inch slices or in spears

1½ cups all-purpose flour

3/8 teaspoon salt

¼ teaspoon pepper

½ teaspoon garlic powder

½ teaspoon onion powder

¼ teaspoon baking powder

1 egg

1 cup milk

1 cup panko bread crumbs

1 cup seasoned bread crumbs

2 cups vegetable oil

Drain the pickles and cut into half-inch slices and pat dry. In a medium bowl, blend the flour, salt, pepper, garlic powder, onion powder and baking powder. In another bowl, stir in the egg and milk together. Mix the panko and seasoned bread crumbs in a bowl.

Heat two cups of oil in a large skillet or fryer to 325°.

Dip each pickle slice in the flour, then egg/milk mixture and press to coat all sides in the panko and breadcrumb mixture. Fry up a few slices at a time until browned on each side, about 30-45 seconds per side.

Serves 3-4

Doah or Dukkah Spice

Use this wonderful spice mixture on pita bread sandwiches, salads, labneh or on top of cream cheese and bagels. All you need is a heavy pan and a food processor to make this addictive spice combo. For a change of taste, you can also add a touch of mint and sumac.

Heat a medium size cast iron pan and add the oil. Add in the sesame seeds and toast to brown lightly, about 3-5 minutes. (Reduce heat if seeds brown too fast). Place the sesame seeds in a large bowl. Then to the pan, in two more batches, toast first the cumin, then the coriander seeds in the same manner. Seeds should be just nicely browned but not charred.

Grind the seeds and spices in a food processor - it will take a while to get the right consistency. Careful - over-processing will result in "doah butter". You're aiming for a fine powder. Season the mixture with salt taste. Keep refrigerated (up to 2 months).

Makes 2½ cups

2-4 tablespoons vegetable oil

2 cups sesame seeds

½ cup cumin seeds

¼ cup coriander seeds

2 teaspoons sea salt

Roasted Garlic Peppers

This is a go-to recipe for green or red peppers, at summer's end which onslaught the market. For a smoky taste, grill over the barbecue. Peppers can also be roasted in a hot oven or broiled over a gas burner. I love these on top of salads or stuffed into sandwiches for added oomph.

6 large peppers (mix of green, red, yellow, and orange)

¼–1/3 cup white or balsamic vinegar

3 large garlic cloves, minced

½ teaspoon salt

Pinch sugar

¼ teaspoon pepper

2/3 cup vegetable or olive oil

2–4 drops liquid smoke, optional

To grill peppers, heat the grill to medium. Prick the peppers all over with a fork. Grill as close to the heat source as possible, turning and rotating the peppers to evenly char (blacken) them on all sides. Peppers should be thoroughly blistered and scorched. Place peppers immediately in a plastic bag and close, allowing peppers to sweat for 15 to 20 minutes. Meanwhile, make the marinade. For oven roasting, preheat oven to 450°. Line a large baking sheet with foil and then line with parchment paper. Prick the peppers all over with a fork and place on the baking sheet. Bake until softened and slightly charred, about 20-30 minutes (taking care to watch them cook so they don't totally blacken)

For the marinade, in a medium bowl, combine vinegar, garlic, salt, sugar, and pepper and then stir in oil and liquid smoke. Remove the charred bits from the peppers and cut them into strips about ½ inch wide.

Toss the pepper strips and cores in the marinade. Using a slotted spoon, transfer the peppers to jars or storage containers and spoon the marinade over them to cover. Serve as an appetizer, in salads, or with cold roast beef and hot mustard.

To store the peppers, refrigerate 2-3 weeks.

Serves 4–6

Brisket Sliders

You'll need an already prepared and cooked brisket (or leftover brisket) to make these fabulous mini sandwiches but other than that, all this appetizer needs is the special sauce here and some small rolls, either slider rolls or homemade mini challah rolls. Pile a platter of these for a Hanukkah part or any occasion. Match this with the Tri Colour Asian Coleslaw in the Beef Chapter along with some caramelized onions and ranch fries or latkes for a holiday feel. I love this appetizer made with BBQ Brisket or the Korean Sriracha Brisket.

Shred the brisket or cut into bite-sized pieces. Place in a large bowl. Prepare rolls by slicing in half. Have a large serving platter nearby.

For the Special Sauce, in a medium saucepan, over medium heat, warm up the pan gravy, BBQ sauce, ketchup, cola, onion powder, smoked paprika, garlic powder and cumin. Season with salt and pepper. Simmer on low for 30 minutes and the pour over brisket in bowl and mix well.

Place bottom half of rolls on platter and top each with 2 ounces or so of the sauced brisket. Top with second half of roll and serve.

Makes 8-10 servings

Brisket Part

4 pounds, approximately, leftover brisket chunks and bite-size pieces

Mini challah rolls, slider or mini hamburger buns

Special Sauce

1 cup pan gravy from brisket, optional

1½ cups honey BBQ sauce

½ cup ketchup

¼ cup cola

½ teaspoon onion powder

½ teaspoon smoked paprika

1 teaspoon garlic powder

¼ teaspoon cumin

Salt, pepper

Chopped Liver and Caramelized Onions

There are some people who can't enjoy chopped liver unless there is a disproportionate amount of onions to liver. This appetizer is more accurately caramelized onions with a garnish of chopped liver. Back in the day, chopped chicken liver included rendered chicken fat which added both flavor and moisture.

Caramelized Onions

6 large onions, thinly sliced in rings

2 tablespoons vegetable oil

Pinch salt, sugar

Liver

5 eggs, hard-boiled

1 pound chicken livers

3 tablespoons oil (or chicken fat)

2 tablespoons finely minced onions

½ teaspoon salt

1/8 teaspoon black pepper

For the caramelized onions, in a 10-12 inch skillet, add the oil and warm up a few minutes on medium heat. Lower heat and add the onions. Slowly sauté the onions, dust with the salt and sugar and cook to brown the onions slowly, 20-40 minutes. Don't rush, allowing the onions all the time they need to become golden brown but don't crisp or scorch. When done, set aside and remove about a third of the onions for the garnish.

For the livers, prepare the hard-boiled eggs While eggs are boiling, in a large non-stick skillet, heat the oil and then add in the chicken liver and raw onions, dusting with salt and pepper. Cook over medium heat until done, (liver is no longer pink inside) about 15 minutes. Cool the liver about 30-40 minutes and then place in a large bowl and chop well by hand with a hand mincer, or in a food processor in pulsing stop/starts to chop but not puree the liver. Take care not to puree it the liver.

Spoon the liver into a medium bowl. Add the half the caramelized onions and the chopped eggs and fold in to blend. Season with salt and pepper. If liver seems too dry, you may add small additional amount of oil and/or chicken stock. Place liver in a serving dish and top with the reserved caramelized onions. Serve with crackers, pita bread, bagels.

Serves 4 to 6

Onion-Kissed Old-Fashioned Potato Knishes

To me nothing beats a simple stretch dough as the easiest dough to work with and one that results in homey-tasting knishes that are good hot or cold. Huge ones are reminiscent of New York street vendor knishes, but small ones are more tender and crisp.

For the mashed potatoes, you will need about 2 pounds peeled potatoes to end up with 4-6 cups mashed potatoes. Peel the potatoes, place in a pot covered with water and bring to the boil. Simmer until fork tender. In a large bowl, mash the potatoes as per your regular method, seasoning with salt, pepper and adding milk (for a dairy meal) or chicken or warm vegetable broth (for a meat meal) to have the right consistency (these are soft mashed potatoes that spread easily as a filling.)

When potatoes are boiling, start the caramelized onions. In a non-stick fry pan, heat the oil slightly and start slowly cooking the onion until they turn golden brown but do not crisp or dry out, about 20 minutes.

For the dough, using a food processor or in a mixer bowl, blend the water, lemon juice, eggs, salt, sugar, and oil and pulse to combine. Add flour and baking powder and process until a smooth mass forms. Add more flour as required. Dough should be smooth, elastic and slack. Remove from work bowl, cover with a damp tea towel and let rest one hour before using. Otherwise, place in a Ziploc bag, refrigerate until required (1-2 days) and allow to warm to room temperature before stretching.

If making this in a stand mixer use the paddle attachment and add the water, lemon juice, eggs, salt and sugar to blend. Add flour and mix until mixture is a mass. Mix on slow speed, until dough is smooth and elastic, adding in only as much additional flour as required to make a soft dough. Cover and let rest 15-30

Stretch Knish Dough

¾ cup warm water

1 teaspoon fresh lemon juice

2 eggs

1 1/8 teaspoon salt

¼ teaspoon sugar

1/3 cup oil

3½ cups all-purpose flour

2 teaspoons baking powder

Mashed Potato filling

4-6 cups mashed potatoes

1 large onion, very finely minced

3 tablespoons oil

Salt, pepper

Egg Wash

2 eggs

¼ cup vegetable oil

minutes (you can also wrap the dough and place in a lightly oiled Ziploc bag and refrigerate up to 2 days). Preheat oven to 350°.

Divide dough in two. On a lightly floured work surface, roll out each section to a 12 by 12 inch rectangle. Spread on half the mashed potatoes and roll up into a log. Using a sharp knife or dough cutter, cut in 15-20 sections. Turn cut side down and press slightly down, gather top cut edge inwards - to form a flower like opening or slight closure (almost as a rose is semi closed)

For the egg wash, in a small bowl, whisk the eggs and oil together.

Stack two baking sheets together and line the top one with parchment paper. Place the knishes on the baking sheet. Brush the knishes all over with egg wash. If you need more, whisk more eggs and oil together. Bake until golden brown, about 25-35 minutes.

Makes 24-35 small to medium knishes

Baba Ganoush

In summer, I grill the eggplants for this recipe on the outdoor barbecue. In winter, I cover the eggplants in foil and grill them over the gas burners of my stove, turning them until the eggplants are softened and the outer skins get charred. A regular oven is also fine for grilling eggplants. My trick is to add a touch of liquid smoke but that's totally optional. This is a heavenly silky dip with a soulful flavor.

Line a baking sheet with foil. Prick the eggplant with fork tines and place on baking sheet.

Bake the eggplant until the skin turns black or very dark brown and juices begin to ooze, 30-45 minutes. Cool well and peel away (and discard) skin. Chop coarsely by hand or in a food processor, and then add the oil, tahini, onion, cumin, coriander, hot sauce, lemon juice, liquid smoke (if using), garlic, salt and pepper. Taste and adjust seasonings as needed. Chill until ready to serve.

Garnish with minced parsley, tomatoes, and red pepper and serve as an appetizer or spread, with dark bread wedges, crackers, or pita.

Serves 4

2 medium eggplants

¼–½ cup light olive oil

¼–1/3 cup tahini

1 tablespoon finely minced onion

2–4 teaspoons cumin

½–1 teaspoon coriander

2–4 drops hot sauce

1/3 cup fresh lemon juice

¼–½ teaspoon liquid smoke, optional

2 large garlic cloves, minced

1 teaspoon salt, or to taste

¼ teaspoon pepper

Finishing Touches

Minced parsley

Minced tomatoes

Minced red pepper

Preheat oven to 400°.

Eggplant Caviar

If you can grill the eggplant outdoors on a barbecue, it makes for a nice smoky flavoured spread. Otherwise, You can also oven bake or microwave the eggplant. This is a smooth, perky tasting starter to any meal, on challah or with crackers.

1 medium to large eggplant

2-3 tablespoons minced onion

1/3 cup light olive oil

¼ cup fresh lemon juice

½ teaspoon kosher liquid smoke seasoning (optional) *

2 large garlic cloves, finely minced

1½ teaspoon salt or to taste

¼ teaspoon pepper

Pinch sugar

Finishing Touches

1/3 cup chopped celery

½ cup chopped tomatoes

3-4 tablespoons chopped scallions

* Liquid smoke comes in a few brands. It is usually available in the soup aisle, or near the condiments and barbecue sauce section in a supermarket.

Preheat the oven to 400°F. Prick the eggplant with fork tines. Place on a foil-lined baking sheet and bake until the eggplant skin blackens, and juices begin to ooze, 35-40 minutes. Cool well, and then peel away skin. Alternatively grill eggplant on an outdoor barbecue, turning often, over coals, wood fire or gas.

Scoop out the eggplant (discard skin) and place in a food processor or a large wood bowl. Chop by hand (with a metal chopper) or in a food processor. The texture should be either puree or slightly lumpy. Stir in remaining ingredients. Adjust seasonings and garnish.

Serve as an appetizer or spread, with dark bread wedges or crackers.

Makes about 2 cups

Smokey Sweet Potato Hummus

What's more sublime than chickpeas, blended with spice and sweet potatoes in an updated hummus? This is a new classic!

Prepare sweet potatoes by simmering in a pot in hot water until tender. Cool and cut in chunks.

Pulse chick peas in food processor to a coarse mash. Add in the sweet potatoes, chick peas, tahini, garlic, salt, pepper, olive oil, cayenne, paprika, cumin, coriander and lemon juice. Pulse to make a paste. Stop machine, adjust seasonings and add some of the reserved chick pea liquid and some additional olive oil if you think the texture requires it. Process again to make a thick, smooth paste.

Chill; then serve on a shallow small dish or platter with pita. Garnish top with minced parsley, mint and cilantro.

Makes 2 cups

2 medium sweet potatoes peeled

1 19 ounce can chick peas drained, with some of the liquid reserved

3 tablespoons tahini

3 garlic cloves, minced

½ to ¾ teaspoon salt

1/8 teaspoon pepper

¼ cup olive oil

¼ teaspoon cayenne

½ teaspoon smoked paprika

1 teaspoon cumin

¼ teaspoon coriander

3-4 tablespoons fresh lemon juice

Finishing Touches

Olive oil

Minced mint, parsley, cilantro

Red Beet Hummus

Hummus doesn't always have to be beige! Now it comes in beautiful hues like pretty orange Sweet Potato Hummus as well as rosy red, like this Red Beet Hummus.

4 medium beets peeled and cubed

5 tablespoons fresh lemon juice

2 tablespoons tahini

2 tablespoons extra virgin olive oil

1 medium garlic clove, minced

1 tablespoon cumin

Zest of one large lemon, finely minced

Salt, pepper

Finishing Touches

2–4 tablespoons minced cilantro

Feta cheese, crumbled

Cucumber slices

Pita bread

Place the beets in a small pot of water and bring to a boil and then simmer until tender, about 20 minutes, drain and cool.

Place the beets in a food processor along with the lemon juice, tahini, olive oil, garlic, cumin, lemon zest, salt, and pepper. Pulse and then process 1-2 minutes to make a smooth paste. Chill until ready to serve.

Serve alongside warm pita bread or spread on cucumber rounds or slices, topped with cilantro and crumbled goat cheese.

Makes 2 cups

North African Hummus

This Northa African chick pea spread, called Bissara, is addictive! It calls for quick and handy, canned fava beans along with touches of dried chili pepper, cumin and a kiss of lemon for a unique, spicy hummus.

Place the fava beans, garlic, olive oil, lemon juice, parsley, chili pepper, paprika, cumin, salt and pepper in a food processor and process 1 to 2 minutes to make a smooth paste. Adjust salt and pepper to taste (or any other seasonings). Chill at least an hour before. Serve with flatbreads or crackers.

Approximately 2 cups

1 19-ounce can fava beans drained

4 garlic cloves, minced

1/3 cup olive oil

2–3 tablespoons fresh lemon juice

3 tablespoons minced parsley

¼ teaspoon dried red chili pepper

2 teaspoons paprika

1-2 teaspoons cumin

Salt, pepper

Golden Beets and Hummus

This is a fabulous recipe that starts with prepared hummus. The visual impact of the golden beets is riveting but the taste of the total package is what makes this a keeper.

3 medium beets, yellow type

¼ cup vinegar

1 teaspoon salt

2 teaspoons sugar

1 cup (prepared) hummus

Finishing Touches

Sprouted chia seeds or watercress

Peel and trim beets and slice about 1/8 inch thin. In a small saucepan, bring some water to the boil. Blanch beets one minute and then put in cold water. Drain. In a medium bowl mix vinegar, salt and sugar and stir in beets to coat.

Serve hummus on a small platter and surround with the beets and top with chia sprouts or watercress. Serve with a rustic bread or fresh pita bread wedges.

Serves 4-6

Sukkot Pumpkin Hummus

With so many varieties of hummus (lentil, beet, sweet potato, to name a few) you don't have to consider a pumpkin hummus just for Sukkot, but it is a nice touch for this fall holiday. Use canned (or fresh pumpkin) but not the pumpkin pie filling. Serve with pita wedges and raw vegetable 'dippers'.

In a food processor, add the drained chickpeas (reserve liquid), pumpkin, tahini, olive oil, lemon juice, cumin, salt and pepper. Process by pulsing for 30 seconds. Taste for taste and texture and add in more oil, chickpea liquid, salt and pepper for taste and the consistency you prefer.

To serve, place in a shallow, small bowl. Make concentric circles with the back of a spoon and drizzle in some olive oil. Garnish with pumpkin seeds, (or sesame) and parsley.

Refrigerate until serving.

Serves 5-6

1 15 oz. can chickpeas

1 cup pumpkin puree

1/4 cup tahini

2 tablespoons olive oil

Juice of 1/2 lemon

1/4 teaspoon cumin

1/4 teaspoon salt

1/8 teaspoon pepper

Finishing Touches

Olive oil

Pepitas, sesame seeds

Minced parsley

Cheese Bourekas

Bourekas are a staple of Turkish cuisine but somehow pops up in the Jewish cooking repertoire, no doubt testimony to how Jewish cooks adapted their roots and culture to dishes they embraced. This is a great appetizer but also good with brunch, dairy-based holidays, or Hanukkah or even as a savory pastry for Purim. Your best bet for folding these would be a YouTube boureka video as they can be made into cigar shapes, coils triangles. You can use knish dough for bourekas, but here I suggest filo or puff pastry.

Dough and Filling

4 sheets filo or half pound puff pastry

½ cup crumbled feta cheese

½ cup grated kashkaval or mozzarella cheese

½ cup drained chopped spinach, optional

1/3 cup ricotta cheese

1 egg

Salt, pepper

Finishing Touches

Egg yolk mixed with 2 tablespoons water

Sesame seeds

Preheat oven to 350°. Stack two baking sheets together and line the top one with parchment paper. In a bowl, combine the cheeses with the egg and season lightly with salt and pepper. Fold in spinach if using.

On a work surface, lay out a piece of filo dough or roll out a section of puff pastry. Cut into 4 by 4 inch squares. Into the center of each, place a tablespoon or so of the filling. Brush edges with egg yolk/water mixture. Fold the dough in half to form a triangle. Place on baking sheet, brush with egg yolk and sprinkle with sesame seeds. Repeat with dough and filling.

Bake until golden brown, 25-35 minutes.

Serve warm (or freeze and reheat)

Makes 36

Chapter Three
Salads and Vegetable Sides

Salads and Vegetable Sides

Salads cover a lot of ground in the Jewish kitchen. They can be regular greens-based salads or related to appetizers in that 'salads' are chilled, vegetables such as marinated eggplant or any Shakshuka variety of pasta, grains, vegetables combined to make something 'salady'. I often find the Jewish table is a bit lacking on hot vegetables (unless it's a vegetarian table) but is rather inventive when it comes to chilled ones.

There's a nice variety of recipes here meant to perk the palate and shift your gaze from starchy (potatoes, rice and pasta) sides as well as adding springy colour to any meal, regardless of season or Jewish holiday. Served a few of these salads at a time and they are a modest feast for the in-between occasions or Jewish holidays. It's all in how you market it.

There are the usual caveats here apply: use fresh, quality vegetables, outstanding oils (whether it's imported olive oil or walnut or non-GMO canola), fresh herbs, spices and the appropriate acidic adds (such as white balsamic vinegar, apple cider or red wine vinegar).

The Sisterhood's Ramen Chicken Salad

This was a huge trend in the '80s that stayed and segued to a classic. But back in the day, it was something you would serve a sisterhood meeting (aka before Facebook), a bridge club or just friends who drop by. Cellophane noodles are also known as Chinese vermicelli or bean thread noodles. They come in a block package of compressed noodles which require about 5 minutes in boiling water to soften.

Soy Chicken Marinade

½ cup soy sauce

2 tablespoons sesame oil

1 tablespoon honey

3 cloves garlic, finely minced

2 tablespoons minced ginger

2 pounds chicken breasts (about 4 large)

Salad Part

3 packets ramen noodles, any flavor

2 to 4 tablespoons toasted sesame oil

1 large package cellophane noodles

2 tablespoons toasted sesame seeds

6 to 12 cups greens such as bok choy, romaine, Napa cabbage, radicchio

1 cup red pepper, slivered

1½ cups steamed, chopped broccoli

2 cups bean sprouts

2 cups sliced mushrooms

½ cup scallions, diced

1 can baby corn, drained and diced

½ cup fresh coriander, coarsely chopped

Asian Vinaigrette

2/3 cup vegetable oil

¼ cup toasted sesame oil

½ cup rice vinegar

Seasoning packets from ramen noodles

¼ cup soy sauce

2 tablespoons peanut butter, optional

½ teaspoon sugar

4 garlic cloves, finely minced

2 teaspoons minced ginger

2 tablespoons fresh lemon juice

Mix Soy Marinade ingredients together. Pour it over the chicken in a small bowl and marinate chicken 1 hour or a few hours (if over an hour, refrigerate).

In a large non-stick skillet, over medium heat, cook the chicken. Add in additional sesame seed oil if mixture dried out while cooking. Cook to sear on side, and the reduce heat and cook other side (about 5-8 minutes). Cut in ¼ inch slivers and set aside.

Break up ramen noodles from soup packet and add to a large bowl. Prepare cellophane noodles by boiling until barely tender in salted water. Drain, rinse with cold water.

To make the Asian Vinaigrette, add all ingredients to a medium bowl and whisk together. Put 1/3 of the dressing in the bottom of the large bowl with the ramen noodles. Place cellophane noodles on top and then all salad ingredients including the chicken. Toss with remaining vinaigrette. Dust with sesame seed and chill for a few hours before serving.

Serves 6

Sukkot Sumac Pita Bread Salad

Ever popular Middle Eastern fattoush salad re-configured for the more spice and vibrant sumac, making this a hearty, rustic and satisfying salad. This is absolutely 'the best' chilled dish ever - definitely more than the sum of the parts. Toss this salad just before serving.

Prepare vinaigrette by combining all ingredients except the olive and vegetable oil. Then drizzle in the two oils, whisking well to combine well. Set aside.

For salad, drizzle olive oil on pita bread, dust generously with salt, pepper, lemon zest and sumac and bake at 350° for 12 to 18 minutes. Cool, and then break into pieces and place in a large bowl.

To the bowl, add everything but the greens and herbs to the bowl. Then add greens but toss just before serving and adding the vinaigrette at this point. Dust with pepper, sumac, parsley, mint and cilantro.

Serves 3-4

Vinaigrette

3 tablespoons red wine vinegar

2 tablespoons balsamic vinegar

1 teaspoon salt

¼ teaspoon sugar

¼ teaspoon pepper

2 teaspoons fresh lemon zest, minced

3 to 4 garlic cloves, minced

½ cup olive oil

¼ cup vegetable oil

Salad

1/3 cup olive oil

4 thick pita breads, cut horizontally

Salt, pepper, sumac

1 pound green beans trimmed, steamed

2 cups grape tomatoes, halved

2 carrots, shredded

1 cup canned white pinto or kidney beans

1 small red onion thinly sliced

½ - 1 cup chevre or feta cheese, in small chunks

4 to 6 cups mixed baby greens

Pepper, sumac, cilantro, parsley, mint, minced

Shatshuka

This is also known as Salad Cuite and it's a North African red pepper, tomato ratatouille or 'stew' that's the quintessential pita mop. If you have some Zhoug on hand, a Yemenite green chili dish, that would be added zest.

¼ cup olive oil

3 medium red peppers, finely diced

1 medium onion, diced fine

1 tablespoon minced garlic

1 28 ounce can ground tomatoes

½ teaspoon salt

¼ teaspoon pepper

¼ teaspoon dry chili flakes

2 teaspoons cumin

1½ teaspoon coriander

1 tablespoon paprika

1 tablespoon fresh lemon juice

1-2 tablespoons Zhoug, optional

Cilantro, parsley, finely minced

In very large non-stick skillet, heat olive oil over medium heat. Add red peppers and cook, lowering heat and stirring to soften, 10-15 minutes. Add in onions and garlic and cook 5 minutes more just to soften onions and garlic. Preheat oven to 325°.

Add canned tomatoes, salt, pepper, chili, cumin, coriander, paprika and lemon juice. Simmer on the stove on very low heat for 30-45 minutes, stirring every so often until mixture thickens and smells very fragrant; season to taste. Serve as a side salad with other cold salads or as a dip with pita bread.

Makes 3-4 cups

Royal Couscous Salad

This is a lemony salad of dueling couscous which includes both the larger Israeli style and the smaller grain one that might be more familiar. This is a really perky dish that goes with almost anything!

Prepare both couscous according to package directions. Place drained, fluffed couscous in a medium bowl. Season with some salt and pepper and mix in the mustard, honey, lemon zest, juice, oil, cucumber, corn, chick peas, red pepper, onion, parsley and cilantro. Toss to blend flavours and ingredients. Taste test for salt and pepper and then refrigerate until serving.

Serves 6-8

1 cup Israeli couscous or pearl couscous

½ cup regular couscous

Salt, pepper

1 teaspoon Dijon mustard

1 teaspoon honey

1 teaspoon minced lemon zest

3 tablespoons fresh lemon juice

¼ cup vegetable oil

1 medium English cucumber, finely diced

1 cup canned corn

1 cup canned chick peas

1 cup red pepper, finely minced

1/3 cup minced green onion

½ cup fresh minced parsley

¼ cup minced cilantro

3 tablespoons minced mint

Persian Cauliflower Rice with Sumac and Pomegranate

I like swaps that work and this one for 'rice' made with cauliflower is a winner. It's very 'rice-like' but a lot less starchy and appealing light but satisfying.

6 cups grated cauliflower

1 cup grape tomatoes, finely diced

2 Persian cucumbers, finely diced

½ cup scallions, finely diced

¾ cup minced parsley

4 tablespoons mint, minced

1 small red onion, finely diced

3 garlic cloves, finely minced

1 teaspoon salt

Juice of 1 lemon

2 tablespoons olive oil

1 tablespoon pomegranate molasses or tamarind paste/molasses

1 teaspoon sumac

Place the grated cauliflower in a large bowl and toss with ¼ cup water. Microwave the cauliflower, stirring every 3-4 minutes until it is slightly tender and softened.

Put the cauliflower in a large bowl. And add remaining ingredients. Refrigerate an hour before serving or overnight.

Serves 6

Smokey Hungarian Potato Salad

This is ideal for cold meals or alongside brisket. It has a decidedly Hungarian Jewish feel to it, given the sultry taste of both sweet and smoked paprika.

Prepare the potatoes by cooking until tender (in their skins). Then cool and slice them in half. Place the potatoes in a large bowl and toss with scallions, onions, mayonnaise, olive oil, red wine vinegar, lemon juice, smoked paprika, sweet paprika and season with salt and pepper. Chill at least an hour before serving.

Serves 6-8

3 pounds fingerlings or small red-skinned potatoes, cooked, sliced in half

½ cup chopped scallions

¼ cup finely chopped red onion

6 tablespoons mayonnaise

3 tablespoons olive oil

1 tablespoon red wine vinegar

1 tablespoon lemon juice

1 teaspoon smoked paprika

2 teaspoons sweet paprika

Salt, pepper

Egyptian Garlic-Lemon Eggplant

I never met an eggplant recipe I didn't like but this marinated, zesty eggplant is my favorite. Whenever you lay out a selection of cold appetizers or salads, this should be there. I use half vegetable and half light olive oil for frying.

Eggplant Part

2 medium eggplants, sliced ¼ inch thin

4 eggs

1½ cups all-purpose flour

Salt, pepper

Vegetable oil

Lemon Vinaigrette

½ cup fresh lemon juice

2–3 garlic cloves, minced

Salt, pepper

Trim the eggplants and slice thin. Dip each in the beaten eggs and then lightly dredge in flour. Lay out on a baking sheet, lined with parchment. Dust with salt and pepper.

Meanwhile, heat up two frying pans with about ½ inch of oil. Fry the eggplant slices, turning once, until tender, a few minutes per side, taking care to brown, but not burn the slices. Drain the slices on paper towels. Arrange all the slices on a large platter.

In a small bowl, whisk together the lemon juice, garlic, cumin salt and pepper. Drizzle the vinaigrette over the eggplant.

Refrigerate at least 2 hours before serving.

Serves 6–8

Old World Grains Salad

This has so many 'good 'grains in it that it is rife with biblical nutrition, aka ancient goodness. Freekeh, an ancient grain, wheat berries, pomegranate seeds, and a honey make this a lovely dish with almost anything but especially fish or a simple roast chicken. I'd serve it for any autumnal Jewish holiday or Tu Bishvat. Freekeh is available in most bulk food stores or from places such as Amazon. It generally comes already toasted' so there's no need to toast the grains prior to cooking.

Place the freekeh and wheat berries in a 4-quart pot, covering with water and bringing to the boil. Cook on medium heat, adding water as needed, on low, checking doneness often, 60-90 minutes until tender but slightly chewy. Fluff up and place in a large bowl. Drizzle with vinegar, honey, olive oil, pomegranate seeds, parsley, pine nuts and goat cheese or feta. Toss and season lightly with salt and pepper.

Serves 4-6

1 tablespoon olive oil

½ cup freekeh

½ cup wheat berries

2 tablespoon balsamic vinegar

1 tablespoon honey

3 tablespoons light olive oil

1 cup fresh pomegranate seeds

2 tablespoons minced parsley

¼ cup pine nuts or chopped walnuts

½ cup goat or feta cheese, in bits

Salt, pepper

Israeli Chopped Layered Salad

This is lovely to look at, crowd-pleasing and handy, as it is can be made ahead up to three days ahead. Marinated, jarred roasted red peppers* speed up the preparation. The trick with this is finely chopped everything so the final result is a pretty, marinated salad you do not have to even toss to serve.

Salad Part

5 hard-boiled eggs, finely chopped

6 cups, chopped mix of green lettuces (such as romaine and iceberg)

½ cup sliced radicchio, finely chopped

1 head, Belgian endive, thinly sliced

1 medium cucumber, finely chopped

1 stalk celery, finely chopped

1 cup shredded carrots

2 medium red peppers, finely chopped *

4 medium tomatoes, finely chopped

1 small red onion, finely chopped

2 scallions, finely chopped

¾ cup black pitted olives, chopped

1½ cups canned beets, finely chopped

Herb Vinaigrette

2 tablespoons fresh lemon juice

1 tablespoon red wine vinegar

2 teaspoons minced garlic

¼ cup mayonnaise

½ teaspoon salt

¼ teaspoon pepper

½ teaspoon basil

½ teaspoon oregano

1 tablespoons minced parsley

½ teaspoon onion powder

½ teaspoon garlic powder

¾ cup light olive oil

¼ cup vegetable oil

Prepare the hard-boiled eggs. Peel and finely chop and set aside. Prepare other vegetables in order given. Using a large serving dish, layer ingredients in order given. Using a plate lightly press ingredients down.

For the Herb Vinaigrette, Add all ingredients, except the olive and vegetable oil to a food processor. Blend one minute. With machine on, slowly drizzle in the oils until mixture thickens, 2-3 minutes. Drizzle vinaigrette over the salad and cover. Refrigerate 2 hours or overnight.

Serves 4-6

Old World Caponata

This is the simplest, sunniest dish you can imagine. You layer on the ingredients – don't bother stirring on the stove – just do this slow oven roast and then dip in! This does double duty as a side salad or dip with bread.

Preheat oven to 350°.

Add everything to a 4-5 quart Dutch oven in order given. Cover and roast, 2-3 hours until vegetables are softened and cooked down, lowering temperature to 325° midway. Alternatively, you can start at 325° and cook it 3-4 hours without temperature adjustment.

Adjust salt and pepper to taste. Serve hot or cold

Serves 6-8

1 large egg plant, washed, trimmed and diced into 1-inch cubes

1 small lemon, washed and thinly sliced

4 medium zucchini trimmed and sliced into ½ inch slices

½ cup pimento stuffed olives, sliced

½ cup pitted black olives, diced

½ cup parsley, finely minced

½ teaspoon dry Italian spices

1 28 ounce can ground or diced tomatoes, preferably plum

Salt, pepper

¼ cup red wine

4 cloves garlic, finely minced

2 tablespoons fresh lemon juice

1/3 cup extra virgin olive oil

Chickpea and Quinoa Salad

Everyone needs at least one chickpea and quinoa salad and this one, lively with North African spices, is a noble offering. I like this for Rosh Hashanah or a bar or bat mitzvah buffet spread.

2 cups cooked quinoa

1 15 ounce chickpeas, drained

1 12 ounce can black beans

1 medium English cucumber, minced

1 medium red pepper, minced

½ cup finely minced red onion

½ cup minced parsley

¼ cup minced cilantro

3 tablespoons lemon juice

1 tablespoon wine vinegar

¼ cup light olive oil

½ teaspoon salt

¼ teaspoon pepper

Prepare the quinoa according to package directions and place it in a medium bowl.

Add the chick peas, black beans, cucumber, red pepper, parsley, cilantro, mint, lemon juice, vinegar, olive oil, salt and pepper and toss to blend. Chill an hour before serving.

Serves 6-8

Farfalle and Feta Cheese Salad

My mother and grandmother always referred to bowtie pasta as farfalle. It was usually served with toasted buckwheat which is the beloved and familiar "Kasha and Bowties". This recipe offers a fresher spin, reconfiguring this dish as a summery pasta-and-grains salad.

Cook the pasta and drain. Place in a serving dish and toss with oil, garlic, red pepper, parsley, green onion and season with salt, pepper and lemon juice. Gently fold in the lemon zest, feta cheese and black olives. Chill an hour before serving.

Serves 6-8

2 cups farfalle or bowtie noodles, cooked

¼ cup olive oil

2 teaspoons finely minced garlic

1½ cups finely minced red pepper

4 tablespoons minced parsley

4 tablespoons minced scallions

Salt, pepper

2 tablespoons fresh lemon juice

2 teaspoons minced lemon zest

1 ½ cups diced feta cheese

¾ cup sliced black olives

Roasted Mediterranean Vegetables

This is both wonderful and easy and a perfect side dish for so many occasions.

4 red-skinned or Yukon Gold potatoes, cut in large wedges

2 Bermuda onions, cut in wedges

1 red onion, sliced ½ inch thick

1 large bulb of garlic, separated and peeled

1 medium eggplant, peeled and in large cubes

2 medium yellow zucchini, in 1-inch chunks

Olive oil

Coarse salt, pepper

Preheat oven to 375°. Have a 6-quart oven casserole or roasting dish ready.

Prepare vegetables (and peel the garlic). Place vegetables in casserole and drizzle with oil (just to coat vegetables nicely). Season with salt and pepper.

Roast until vegetables are softened, about 45 – 60 minutes, or as required.

Serves 6-8

Roasted Cauliflower with Kale and Sumac

Cauliflower is a classic now getting a bit more attention. Sumac, olive oil and the caramelization that occurs in roasting makes this a center piece 'side'. For a variation, ditch the sumac and use smoked paprika instead or any spice approach you prefer.

Preheat oven to 400°. Line a baking sheet with parchment paper. Prepare kale and drizzle with a bit of olive oil. Place in oven, reduce temperature to 375°, and bake until softened, 15-20 minutes. Remove and then place the cauliflower on the baking sheet. Drizzle with olive oil and lemon juice. Then dust with salt, pepper and sumac.

Bake until tender, 45 minutes.

Serves 6

1 head of kale, washed, spines removed

Olive oil

1 medium cauliflower, cored and trimmed

¼ cup olive oil

Salt, pepper, sumac

Juice of half a lemon

Chapter Four
Soups

Soups

It's a given that most cultures would claim bragging rights on the comforts of soup and their iconic recipes in particular. That said, no one disputes the curative powers of Jewish "chicken soup. As evidenced by the meme it's become, Jewish Chicken Soup and Matzoh Balls seems to reign supreme as quintessential soup of record. It's the classic 'you don't have to be Jewish' joke in that you really don't have to be Jewish to enjoy Jewish Chicken Soup and all the warmth and care that is part and parcel of the recipe. You don't even have to be a meat eater because I've provided a vegan version of Jewish Chicken Soup! And for those that want their chicken soup to be a bit more cutting edge? I've created Kosher Pho which is 'chicken soup' with upbeat Vietnamese notes of lemon grass, ginger, mint and basil.

Chicken soup is just the beginning. In the Jewish kitchen, soup can be a lot of things from cold, refreshing beet borscht (borscht meaning *soup* in Russian) served with a dollop of sour cream or (more trendy) Greek yogurt, a hearty deli-style Bean, Mushroom and Barley or a Sephardic Spicy Lentil Soup.

Most of my soup recipes are vegetarian-based. I approached my soups this way because I believe using a vegetable base, even while I strove to keep the keep the flavours bold and vibrant, let soups do double duty. For one thing, they're wonderfully staying soups for any meal but their vegetarian approach allows you (if you're observant) to serve your soup with a meat or dairy meal, and/or if you're vegetarian (or friends and family are), you can also enjoy the soup.

Of course, on occasion, one wants a healthy bone broth or meat-based soup and I've included a couple of those as well. Soup bones and tough cuts of meat like flanken contain a host of nutrients that meat- eating folks enjoy and are also flavor boosters.

The thing to remember about making a great soup is to use a superlative, quality stock pot – something nicely heavy bottomed so if you do include any pulses (lentils, peas, beans) or grains (barley, rice), there's a lesser chance that things will scorch or stick at the bottom and clean up is easier. Number two is to use fresh herbs (but quality dry herbs are more than adequate) and the most potent of spices. Check your spices every few months or so. Spices are inexpensive, so there's no point ruining a good batch of soup with sub-standard or old, muted spices. Number three is my recommendation that you use spring or filtered water. Water is 90% of what your soup is made of, so you might as well go the distance and invest in 'better' water. At the least, depending on where you live, if you use spring water, you won't be adding chlorine bleach to your beautiful soup!

Salt and Pepper to Taste?

Salt and pepper are so ubiquitous in cooking, especially soup that we generally take them for granted. But there are so many salts: kosher, sea salt, fleur de sel and others. There's also the magic of gourmet-fragrant Tellicherry peppercorns. Since soup is all about savory perfection, take the time to consider which salt and which pepper you prefer, because it does make a difference. If you are in any doubt of which is best, just do your own taste test. Grind up some salt or have a few fine salts on hand and taste them. You will be amazed at the character (or lack thereof) in this ingredient (and ditto for pepper). Try a supermarket pepper alongside a specialty spice house pepper. Invariably, it is the difference between freshly ground pepper 'dust' and totally vibrant, brisk, zesty, heat and spice-laden great pepper.

Soups, like all else in the kitchen of wholesome food, is a series of little things done well. So, make sure the basic elements are chosen with care. It is those little touches that separate good homemade soup from superlative elixirs and gourmet potions.

One more soup trick! Sour Salt or Citric Acid

The secret 'zap' and perk of so many soups

Sour salt or citric acid are interchangeable names for a dry, white granular powder, much like salt or sugar, that I use in soups, lemony things (such as my recipe for Lemon Bars), and anything that requires a real hit of acidic punch. This is especially worth noting for recipes wherein I don't want to 'lemon' up in flavor nor add too much liquid, but I want the tartness to shine through. Be careful however, a little citric acid or sour salt goes a long way! Most times, just a pinch will do. You can find citric acid online or in the kosher food section of some stores. Tartaric acid is another granular substance. Similarly, acidic as citric acid is, it's scraped from the inside of wine casks. It is the acidic residue that forms, becomes crystalline, and then can be scraped off to be converted into tartaric acid and used whenever citric acid is called for. This is an ingredient well worth seeking out, especially for the recipe for Cabbage Soup that is beautifully sweet and sour.

So…did I mention that soup and appetizers are in fact a meal? Did I mention that soups freeze well? Did I mention that nothing tastes better than a hunk of pumpernickel alongside a bean soup? I guess I just did! Happy soup-making!

How to Make Perfect Chicken Soup

Sometimes people forget that wonderful, simple things are but a series of little steps, each carefully and caringly followed. Good food is all in the details. Understanding how to create an outstanding Jewish Chicken Soup with Matzoh Balls exemplifies this 'all in the details' like nothing else I know.

For starters, a kosher chicken for a great Jewish chicken soup is a must. For years, I used regular chickens and made (I thought) rather good soup. And then one day, while home with sniffles, a caring friend brought me her homemade soup. It was jaw-droppingly good. Far better than mine! What was the difference? Kosher chicken!

Kosher chicken soup has this full bodied flavour that cannot be replicated any other way (although this recipe is so good you could make it with a too-mature capon and it would still taste terrific). Next, you need a good-sized chicken –nothing is worse than watery chicken soup that you try and remedy by adding too much salt. Salt is imperative. Kosher salt, which is iodine free, offers the purity of taste you want.

My *last* trick, for a very pretty soup, is to drain off the stock pot vegetables (i.e. the carrots, parsnips, and greens). As the soup heats and the matzoh balls are added, put new carrots and some fresh parsley and dill in. These stay fresher looking and are far more colourful.

For the Matzoh Balls recipe, my recommendation is to separately poach them in salted water. If you poach them in the chicken soup itself, the flavour is incomparable but the matzoh balls will soak up a lot of the precious stock. I add some pepper and dill to the salted water and simmer the matzoh balls until ready. Once ready, they are drained and gently lowered into the chicken soup.

Matzoh Balls – Hard or Soft?

There are many variations on matzoh balls, also known as kneidlach, which is a Yiddish word for dumplings. Some cooks add a touch of ginger, fresh herbs, or baking powder (which is omitted during Passover, of course) to their matzoh balls, giving it a unique touch, which becomes family culinary legacy. Others add a touch of broth, water or seltzer water or vary the ratio of eggs and oil to the matzoh meal. Other matzoh ball makers debate whole eggs simply blended in or separating the eggs and folding. No matter how you make your matzoh balls, you will have fans and others who compare them to another version. It's all good, even the convenient boxes of commercial matzoh ball mix which is the 'secret' a lot of great cooks use!

Classic Chicken Soup and Matzoh Balls

This classic deli-and-home chicken soup and a proven cold remedy gets the Jewish Food Hall of Fame award. It's iconic! Both kosher chicken and kosher salt make a huge difference here but I guarantee you, even a 'regular' chicken and regular salt in this recipe will yield an incomparable soup.

Finishing Touches

1-2 cup carrots, sliced

1 cup chopped celery

Fresh minced parsley, dill

Matzoh balls

Soup

1 3-4 pound chicken, preferably kosher

1 pound chicken legs and wings

Water just to cover chicken (approximately 14-16 cups)

1 tablespoon black peppercorns

1 tablespoon salt

2 large stalks celery

2 large carrots, scraped, cut into chunks

2 parsnips scraped, cut in chunks

1 medium onion peeled, halved

½ cup parsley, minced

½ cup fresh dill, coarsely chopped

Salt, pepper

Rinse the chicken well. Place the chicken (and extra parts) in a 12-quart stock pot. Cover with cold water that should just cover top of chicken.

Bring water to a boil, skimming off any foam that forms. Reduce to a medium simmer; add the peppercorns, salt, celery, carrots, parsnips, onion, parsley, and dill. Cover partially and simmer for 2-3 hours. When the soup is done, taste for salt and pepper and add if required. Let the soup cool an hour before straining it. Strain off everything but the soup. (Save choice chicken pieces for chicken salad filling or to add back smaller strips or pieces of soup chicken to the pot). Add in the carrots, parsley and dill.

When ready to serve soup, add 1-2 matzoh balls per serving

Serves 12-14

Matzoh Balls

These are the quintessential dumplings that sit like lofty mountains in puddles of hot, fragrant chicken soup. Matzoh balls, hard or soft (everyone has a preference), are what make the holidays, 'the holidays' and what make Jewish chicken soup a meal in itself.

1 cup matzoh meal

½ teaspoon salt

1/8 teaspoon pepper

½ teaspoon baking powder, optional *

4 eggs

2 tablespoons chicken soup stock or water

1/3 cup vegetable oil

* The baking powder is optional and to be omitted at Passover.

Place the matzoh meal in a medium bowl along with the salt, pepper and baking powder. Add the eggs, chicken soup and oil. Blend well with a spoon and let stand at room temperature or refrigerate two minutes or until mixture is firm enough that you can handle it and form into matzoh balls.

Fill a Dutch oven three quarters full of water and 2 teaspoons of salt. Bring to a rolling boil. With wet or oiled hands (latex gloves are great for messy kitchen jobs like this) scoop matzoh ball mixture, forming into balls about 2-3 inches diameter. Gently drop into boiling water; reduce heat, cover pot and let the matzoh balls simmer 30 minutes.

Gently remove matzoh balls from water and drain. Gently ladle into the chicken soup. Serve 1-2 matzoh balls per serving.

10-14 matzoh balls

Kosher Pho

Pho is a wonder soup! No wonder it's a trend that is now well ensconced as a classic. Nothing beats this tempting Vietnamese soup, and nothing is lost in making it kosher. The recipe makes a big batch and you will bless yourself (and me) on a chilly day when you find yourself cold and tired and don't know what to eat. This will be perfect. It calls for Maggie Seasoning which is found in the soup section of most supermarkets. It adds an umami flavor that makes it really authentic.

Chicken Poaching Part

4 pounds chicken parts

Water to cover chicken

Soup Part

4 pounds chicken (reserved from poaching)

6 quarts water

1-2 tablespoons salt

2 tablespoons coriander seeds

6 whole cloves

8 Thai chili peppers

½ teaspoon Maggie seasoning

1½ teaspoon grated rock or palm sugar or brown sugar

3 large onions, quartered (peel on)

1 6-inch chunky piece ginger root, unpeeled

1 tablespoon vegetable oil

Add-Ins

Cooked rice noodles

Scallions sliced

Mint leaves

Fresh cilantro

Cucumber strips

Carrot strips

Lemon grass

Star anise

Bean sprouts

Sesame seed oil

Lime slices

In a 12-quart saucepan, barely cover the chicken with water. Bring to a rapid boil and let cook five minutes. Drain the liquid and keep the chicken. Rinse the pot briefly and then put the chicken back in. Cover with 6 quarts of water and slow heat up.

Meanwhile, in a cast iron skillet, heat the vegetable oil. Slowly cook the onions and ginger to brown or slightly scorch, about 5-10 minutes. This makes the onion and ginger very aromatic. Remove and trim off scorched parts. Then add ginger and onions to soup. Add the salt, coriander seeds, chili peppers and let soup simmer one hour; adjust seasonings. Serve soup with some rice noodles in each bowl. Garnish with shreds of the cooked chicken, and mint leaves, cilantro, cucumber and carrots strips. Otherwise, let it cool in the fridge overnight and drain it so that you have a clear soup, reserving the best chicken for the soup or for a salad or whatever you like.

Serves 8-10

Old Fashioned Mushroom Bean and Barley Soup

This soup is a nice alternate to Chicken Soup on a Shabbat winter night. Some people add flanken, aka lean pieces of beef that make this a whole-meal soup but I prefer it vegetarian style.

1 1-ounce package Polish or European dehydrated mushrooms

12 cups spring water, or beef or chicken stock

3 tablespoons unsalted butter or vegetable oil

4 cups fresh mushrooms, finely sliced

1 small rib celery, finely chopped

1 medium carrot, finely chopped

1 medium onion, finely chopped

1 small garlic clove, finely minced

2/3 cup pearl barley

½ cup dried lima or navy beans

¼ cup yellow dried split peas

2 tablespoons parsley, finely minced

1 teaspoon onion powder

2 teaspoons paprika

1 teaspoon salt or to taste

¼ teaspoon pepper

1 tablespoon fresh lemon juice

Place the dried mushrooms in a small bowl and cover with steaming water. Let stand 20 minutes, reserve liquid and remove mushrooms and finely chop.

Meanwhile, in a 6-quart stock pot, heat the butter or oil over low heat and sauté the mushrooms until slightly softened, stirring often, about 5-8 minutes. If mushrooms stick, add in a touch more oil and a few tablespoons of water to enable them to sauté and not scorch. Add in the celery, carrot and onion and continue to cook to soften (but not brown), stirring often. Stir in the garlic and cook briefly. Add in the reserved mushroom liquid and chopped dried mushrooms, the barley, beans, peas, parsley, onion powder and paprika, some salt and pepper. Stir in the lemon juice.

Bring to gentle bubble and then immediately lower the heat and let the soup simmer 90 minutes or until beans and barley are softened, stirring every so often and making sure nothing sticks to the bottom of the pot. The soup is ready when the beans and barley are totally softened. Adjust seasonings. If you like, you can puree half the soup so that you have a hearty thick broth with just enough chunkier bits for visual interest. This keeps for a few days in the refrigerator and also freezes well. When reheating, heat slowly, drizzling in more water slowly to loosen soup (beans and barley soups will thicken once they are refrigerated)

6-8 servings

Old Country Pea Soup

This hearty soup is summer time fresh, with carrots, celery and dried split peas. You can also add 1-2 tablespoons barley for a heartier soup. A touch of margarine (or butter) makes an essentially vegetarian soup a little 'meatier' and is a kosher trick from back in the day when housewives would slip in a dollop or margarine to get that 'meaty' taste in a pareve soup.

Bring peas and water to a boil. Skim off foam and reduce heat to simmer and add onions, carrots, celery, parsley, celery powder, salt, pepper. Cook until peas are softened (about 45 minutes) then add potato cubes and continue cooking over low to medium heat until peas are completely dissolved, about 1½ hours).

Stir to blend soup. Adjust seasonings, stir in butter or oil, adjusting salt, pepper and dill to taste. Reheat on very low heat.

Serves 10-12

12 cups water

2 cups yellow or green split peas

¾ cup chopped onions

2 cups sliced carrots

1 cup diced celery

¼ cup minced fresh parsley

1/8 teaspoon celery seed powder

2-4 teaspoons salt

1 teaspoon pepper

3 medium potatoes, peeled and cubed

2 tablespoons butter or olive oil (optional)

The Paprika Restaurant Cream of Cauliflower Soup

A quaint, now gone, little Hungarian restaurant in my town called The Paprika used to serve this soup as their specialty. On a busy night, they must have gone through troughs of this simple, satisfying cauliflower soup wonder. If you have some sweet, imported Szeged Hungarian paprika on hand, that would be the perfect touch.

1 large cauliflower cut into small chunks and florets

¼ cup unsalted butter or vegetable oil

1 medium onion, finely diced

1 medium clove garlic, finely minced

1 large potato, peeled and diced

1 small carrot, finely shredded

3 tablespoons flour

1 tablespoon sweet paprika such as Szeged, or similar quality imported paprika

Salt, pepper

½ teaspoon dried dill weed

1 cup warm milk

4 cups warm chicken stock

2 cups warm water

½ cup sour cream or Greek yogurt

In a large pot, blanch the cauliflower in boiling water about 5 minutes, remove and drain.

In a large stock pot, heat the butter or oil over medium heat. Add and sauté the onions to soften 5-10 minutes. Add the garlic to briefly soften but not brown, 2-3 minutes. Add the cauliflower, potato and shredded carrots. Cook to soften vegetables, stirring often, about 12-15 minutes.

Sprinkle on the flour and paprika, salt, pepper and the dill weed, tossing to cook the flour about 5 minutes. Slowly drizzle in the milk, chicken stock and water and stir.

Cook over low heat, about 45 minutes. Puree in a food mill, food processor or immersion blender and then return to the pot. Using a whisk, stir in sour cream, very briskly stirring. Adjust seasonings.

Serves 6-10

Vegetarian Minestrone Soup

Some restaurants make this ho-hum, which is a pity when it is a favorite classic and can be so exciting and satisfying. I think my home version of this Italian restaurant staple is outstanding and fortifying. This recipes uses citric acid or sour salt (but if you leave it out the recipe is still exceptional).

3 tablespoons olive oil

3 tablespoons water

4 medium garlic cloves, minced

½ cup diced onions

1½ cups sliced carrots

1 cup chopped celery

2 cups finely shredded cabbage

1 cup diced zucchini

1 28-ounce can crushed tomatoes

16 cups water

1 cup mixed dried beans (Romano, kidney, fava, pinto, cranberry, etc.)

¼ cup whole dried peas

1 to 3 tablespoons pearl barley

1½ tablespoons salt

1-2 tablespoons sugar

1 teaspoon pepper

½ teaspoon hot sauce

¾ teaspoon garlic powder

2 bay leaves

2 teaspoons oregano

2 teaspoons basil

1 teaspoon celery seed

¼ cup minced fresh parsley

¼ teaspoon crushed red pepper

2 tablespoons red wine

¼ to ½ teaspoon citric acid or sour salt *

(*) Citric acid, tartaric acid or sour salts - available in ethnic food stores or larger drug stores. Substitute 4-8 tablespoons of fresh lemon juice

In a 12-quart stock pot, heat the oil and water briefly, add the garlic, onions, carrots, celery, cabbage, zucchini and over low heat, sauté until are softened, 10-20 minutes. Add water, crushed tomatoes, dried beans, peas, barley, salt, sugar, pepper, Tabasco, garlic powder, bay leaves, oregano, basil, celery seed, parsley, red pepper, wine and citric acid. Simmer, semi-covered, 2-3 hours until beans are soft. Adjust seasonings.

Serve with fresh Parmesan cheese, cooked bite-sized pasta and homemade garlic croutons or Italian bread.

Serves 12-16

Old Country Style Lentil Soup

What's nice about this soup is that it is not heavily spiced in one tradition or another, so I consider it a 'crossroads' between gourmet health food cafe and East European.

3 tablespoons light olive oil

3 cloves garlic, finely minced

1 small onion, finely minced

1½ cups minced carrots

½ cup finely minced celery

1 cup lentils either brown or green (or mixed)

2-3 tablespoons barley

3 tablespoons tomato paste

½ cup celery leaves, coarsely chopped

1 bay leaf

2 cup spinach, (or Swiss Chard) coarsely chopped, optional

1 teaspoon garlic powder

1 teaspoon onion powder

1 tablespoon paprika

¼ cup parsley, finely minced

Salt, pepper

8 -10 cups chicken stock or vegetable stock

1 tablespoon balsamic or red wine vinegar

1 tablespoon lemon juice

2 small potatoes peeled and cut in ½ inch dice

½ cup canned cooked chicken peas

1 cup small cubes (peeled) squash

In a 6-quart stock pot, heat the olive oil and sauté the garlic, onion, carrots, and celery for 5-10 minutes on low.

Stir in the lentils, barley, tomato paste, celery leaves, bay leaf, spinach, garlic powder, onion powder, paprika, parsley, a little salt and pepper. Stir briefly and add in the chicken stock, vinegar and lemon juice. Simmer 1-2 hours until barley is almost softened. Add in potatoes, chick peas and squash and simmer until barley is softened. Season to taste.

5-6 Servings

Country Pea and Carrot Soup

One of my all-time favorites, go-to recipes; it's fast and easy and satisfying (and vegetarian if you use olive oil). This is the signature soup of my mother-in-law, Shirley Posluns.

Bring peas and water to a boil. Skim off foam and reduce heat to simmer. Add onions, carrots, celery, parsley, dill, celery seed, salt, and pepper. Cook until peas are softened (about 45 minutes) then add potato cubes and continue cooking over low to medium heat until peas are completely dissolved (approximately 1½ hours).

Stir to blend soup. Adjust seasonings, stir in butter, adding more salt, pepper and dill to taste. Reheat on very low heat. Freezes well.

Serves 12-14

12 to 14 cups water

2 cups yellow or green split peas

¾ cup finely chopped onions

2 cups sliced carrots

1 cup diced celery

¼ cup minced fresh parsley

1-2 tablespoons fresh dill or 1 tablespoon dried

1-2 teaspoon celery seed

2-4 teaspoons salt

¾ teaspoon pepper

3 medium potatoes, peeled and cubed

2 tablespoons unsalted butter (optional)

Finishing Touches

Cooked noodles (any shape or size), optional

Fresh minced parsley

Classic Cream of Leek and Potato Soup

Can this feast be a mere soup? No matter what you do with leeks, to cook with them is to acquire instant sophistication. Rich enough for a meal or afternoon snack and comforting enough to upstage hallowed chicken soup. Nice with French bread and a wedge of blue cheese and Bosc or Anjou pears for Shabbat luncheon or Shavuot.

¼ cup unsalted butter (or part olive oil)

2 large garlic cloves, finely minced

6 large leeks, trimmed and sliced into ½ inch slices *

2 scallions, finely diced

1 tablespoon minced chives

2 large shallots, finely minced

4 medium potatoes, peeled and diced

3 tablespoons flour

2 cups warm chicken stock

3 cups warm milk

¼ cup white wine

2-4 tablespoons fresh parsley, finely minced

Salt, pepper

In an 8-quart stock pot, melt the butter. Sauté the garlic, leeks, scallions, chives and shallots until softened, over low heat, about 10-15 minutes. Add the potatoes and sauté to soften and cook potatoes, another 15-20 minutes. Stir often and season with salt and pepper. Dust on flour and stir to coat, 2-3 minutes.

Add in the chicken stock, warm milk, white wine and parsley. Simmer over lowest possible heat (or milk will curdle). Stir, simmer and adjust seasonings.

Cool down, then sieve through a food mill or puree in batches via your food processor or a blender. Return to soup pot and heat on low.

Serves 6-8

Deli Style Mushroom, Bean and Barley Soup

After chicken soup, this is a deli staple. Soak the beans overnight, just covered in water to get a head start. If you don't have time or forethought to do that, just let the soup simmer longer as required until the beans are tender.

The night before, or a few hours, cover the beans with spring water in a medium bowl and let stand. At the same time, in a small bowl, soak mushrooms in approximately ½ cup water. Drain the water from the mushrooms but reserving the liquid.

In a large 6 to 8-quart stock pot, heat the oil to low-medium and sauté the garlic, onion, celery and carrots until lightly browned and softened. Stir in the stock or water, barley, lima beans, salt, pepper, parsley, paprika and add the drained mushrooms. Bring to a boil, and then reduce heat to simmer. Cook, stirring occasionally, until beans are cooked (3 to 4 hours). Adjust seasonings and add water if soup has thickened too much.

You may have to add more water and spices later if soup thickens after being refrigerated as well. Reheat soup on low heat.

Serves 6-8

½ cup dried lima beans

4 tablespoons (about ½ ounce) imported dried mushrooms

4 tablespoons light olive oil

2 garlic cloves, minced

1 cup minced onions

½ cup chopped celery

½ cup finely chopped carrots

2 quarts hot chicken or vegetable stock (or water)

½ cup pearl barley

Salt, pepper

2 tablespoons minced parsley

½ teaspoon paprika

Russian Sweet and Sour Cabbage Soup

This bold and hearty soup can scare the chill away with the first spoonful! Pair it with Russian black bread for a satisfying meal. If you like, add some beef bones if you have them on hand and want a meat-based soup. I also like this with mini potato kugels.

1 cup water

3 tablespoons vegetable oil

1 medium cabbage, finely shredded

2 medium onions thinly sliced and minced

1 large clove garlic, minced

1 large carrot, thinly sliced and minced

1 cup light brown sugar

¼ - ½ cup white sugar

10 cups water, or more, as required

1 28 ounce can crushed tomatoes

1 10 ounce can tomato soup

2 tablespoons tomato paste

1-2 tablespoons caraway seeds

1-2 tablespoons salt

½ - 1 teaspoon pepper

1-2 teaspoons citric acid or 2 tablespoons lemon juice

(*) Citric acid, tartaric acid, or sour salts bring the sour to sweet-and-sour. Available in ethnic food stores and some drug stores. You may substitute juice of two lemons or to taste.

In a 10-12-quart stock pot, add about a cup of water and oil. Over medium heat sauté the cabbage, onions, garlic and carrot with the brown and white sugar until lightly golden and softened.

Stir in water, crushed tomatoes, tomato soup, tomato paste, caraway seeds, salt, black pepper and citric acid (*). Simmer on medium, reducing heat to low as required, for 2 to 2½ hours. Adjust seasonings, adding additional amounts of sugar, salt, citric acid and caraway seeds for a more pronounced sweet and sour taste. Serve with a dollop of sour cream or yogurt, parsley and caraway seed garnish.

Serves 12-14

Sweet Paprika Smokey Bean Soup or Bableves

A hearty pinto bean soup that sticks to your ribs. You can use any sort of dried beans for this soup and add 1-2 tablespoons of barley to make it a bit more rustic. When I make this soup without meat, I add a few drops of liquid smoke for flavour or I add in slices of smoked turkey sausage.

Place beans in a medium saucepan and cover with cold water one inch over the beans. Bring to a boil and let boil gently for 12-15 minutes. Remove and drain.

Place beans in an 8-quart pot. Add the water along with onion, green pepper, garlic, carrot, celery, paprika, liquid smoke, hot sauce, salt and pepper. Bring to a gentle boil, reduce heat and let simmer until beans are softened. Add the turkey sausages (if using) and simmer 20-30 minutes to develop flavours.

In a separate skillet, make a roux by heating up butter or olive oil and adding the flour. Stir to cook flour and allow it to thicken and brown. Stir this into warm soup, along with the tablespoon of vinegar. Adjust seasonings and add a touch more water if necessary (i.e. soup gets too thick).

Serves 8-10

1 cup dried pinto beans

8-10 cups water

1 medium onion, finely diced

1 green pepper, diced

2 cloves garlic, minced

1 large carrot, thinly sliced

2 medium ribs celery, finely chopped

1 tablespoon paprika

¼-½ teaspoons Liquid Smoke, optional

3-6 drops hot sauce

Salt, pepper

1-2 turkey sausages sliced, optional

2 tablespoons butter or olive oil

3 tablespoons flour

1 tablespoon vinegar

Chapter Five
Potatoes, Rice, Noodles and
Grains

Potatoes, Rice, Noodles and Grains

It's easy to make the same starches over and over again. Who doesn't get hooked on this traditional venue of comfort foods. Nothing is as easy, fool-proof, crowd-pleasing (these sorts of recipes make a little or a lot in short work) as a great potato (or rice or noodle side). Starches, especially the humble potato, isn't usually considered haute cuisine. The potato/starch connection is decidedly peasant fare but it's always tasty, staying and adaptive to whatever else you're serving. There's just something about rustic potatoes and well-made rice that speak to the spirit and soul. Pair up a great potato, noodle or rice dish to a chicken main you have simple food that speaks volumes in the lexicon of comfort food.

This chapter leans on the potato end of things (both regular potatoes and sweet potatoes) but it is also home to (bringing in the East Euro connection), varenikas, kreplach and some biblical grains like home style kasha and bow ties.

We too often shun carbohydrates as some sort of dietary evil, but the truth is they both anchor and frame the meal. Carbs, especially these crafted recipes from the Jewish kitchen, are substantive and while modest, deserving of respect. They are also, for a good part, either traditional or have an historical tie so put aside your carb-prejudices and jump in. They are great for daily fare or holiday times, are make-head perfect, reheat (or freeze) beautifully and are part of the continuum of the Jewish food railways.

Friday Night Roasted Lemon Potatoes

In the East European style of Jewish cuisine, you can never have to many high-performance but easy potato side-dish recipes. This one is one of my go-to recipes. It goes with so many main dishes (chicken, beef or fish) and there's never any leftovers.

Peel the potatoes and place in a 4-5 quart pot and cover with water. Bring to a boil until barely tender (par boil) about 10-12 minutes. Drain with cold water. Cut potatoes into quarters.

In a large, non-stick fry pan, warm the oil over medium heat and then add the potatoes and gently fry, dusting with salt and pepper as they cook.

If you prefer not to fry, place the oil, potatoes, and remaining ingredients in a 9 by 13 inch roasting pan and bake them, until they brown (tossing every once in awhile), for 40-60 minutes.

Serves 3-4

6-8 medium large red-skinned potatoes

½ cup light olive oil

Salt, pepper

4-6 cloves garlic, finely minced

Juice half a lemon

3 tablespoons white wine

1/3 cup minced parsley

1 lemon, sliced

Persian Rice with Potato Tahdig

Jewish cuisine really has no borders save the laws of Kashrut. Consequently, 'my' Jewish kitchen includes many international influences, showcasing my preference for flair in flavors. I first learned recipe for Persian Rice when I worked in a health food store in the beginning of my career where I was the head baker and two Iranian sisters did the salads and rice honours. I was fascinated by the method and the notion of two starches (rice and potatoes) as well as the concept of the potatoes on the pot bottom acting as a steaming 'rack'. The taste was out of this world! This would be lovely for the High Holidays or Passover.

Pinch saffron threads

1 cup hot water

2 cups basmati rice

2 teaspoons salt

Vegetable or light olive oil (for pot)

3 large potatoes such as Yukon Gold or Potomac, peeled and sliced ¼ inch

4 tablespoon light olive oil or butter

In a small bowl, place the saffron and cover with the hot water.

Prepare the potatoes place in a bowl; cover with cold water. Meanwhile, rinse the rice 2-3 times or until the water runs clear. Place the rice in a large pot of water (to cover rice) with the salt and boil gently for 10-12 minute to tenderize and then rinse with cold water and drain.

In the bottom of the pot smear with the oil. Drain the potatoes and add to the bottom of the pot. Wider pots accommodate the potatoes better, but if you have to double stack them, that's fine.

Season with a little salt and pepper and then gently spoon the semi-cooked rice on top and add saffron-water on top of that. Poke holes in the rice with a chopstick and add in the oil or bits of the butter. Place a tea towel on the rim of the pan and then cover it. Simmer on lowest heat possible, about 45-60 minutes until rice is thoroughly cooked. Fluff rice a bit before removing, and then invert onto a serving place (potato slices should be browned and sticking to rice).

Serves 4-5

Chicken Kreplach

Kreplach are a form of filled dumplings, triangular, thin and delicate, and filled with chicken (or beef, mushroom, spinach, kasha or cheese filling) you can serve in soup (not the cheese ones) or as a side dish or appetizer. The trick is to roll the dough thin or if you're time-pressed, you can use egg roll wrappers. Kreplach can be boiled or boiled and then lightly fried in schmaltz or oil with browned onions.

For the Kreplach Dough, mix flour, water, eggs and salt in a medium bowl by hand, kneading gently until a soft dough forms. Cover and set aside.

For the filling, in a small frypan over medium heat, brown the onion in the oil until golden, about 8-10 minutes. Place the chicken in a medium bowl and add the onions, salt, pepper and parsley and mix well.

To prepare the kreplach, in a lightly floured board, roll out half the dough as thinly as possible. Cut into 3-inch circles. Place a tablespoon of filling in the center of the circle and paint edges of dough with water (as a glue) Either fold over the dough to form a triangle or fold, as you would for hamantashen, fold into the middle to make a three-cornered filled dumpling. Repeat with dough and filling.

Meanwhile, in a 4-quart pot, bring 4-5 cups of water and a teaspoon salt to a low boil. Add in kreplach a few at a time and cook 15-20 minutes. Remove. Serve as a dish or add to chicken soup instead of matzoh balls.

Makes 24

Kreplach Dough

2 cups all-purpose flour

2-3 tablespoons water

2 eggs

½ teaspoon salt

Chicken Kreplach Filling

¼ cup finely minced onion

2 tablespoons vegetable oil

1 ½ cups cooked chicken soup chicken, finely chopped

½ teaspoon salt

¼ teaspoon pepper

1 tablespoon finely minced parsley

Rosemary Asiago Potato Knishes

You gotta admit that some classics take especially well to innovation and this is one such. These knishes are a great snack or side (for a non-meat meal) and the touches of rosemary and asiago upgrade the onion-deli approach usually found in delis. Feel free to substitute whatever cheese you prefer. The small chunk of cheese nestles inside and once found, you get a treat of molten cheese and potato filling encased with the traditional stretch deli dough.

Stretch Knish Dough

¾ cup warm water

1 teaspoon lemon juice

2 eggs

1 1/8 teaspoon salt

¼ teaspoon sugar

1/3 cup oil

3½ cups all-purpose flour

2 teaspoons baking powder

Mashed Potato Asiago Filling

4-6 cups mashed potatoes *

1 medium onion, finely minced

3 tablespoons oil

1-2 tablespoons minced fresh rosemary

Salt, pepper

Milk or vegetable broth, as required

24-36 1-inch chunks Asiago cheese

Egg Wash

2 eggs

¼ cup vegetable oil

For the mashed potatoes, you will need about 2 pounds peeled potatoes to end up with 4-6 cups mashed potatoes. Peel the potatoes, place in a pot covered with water and bring to the boil. Simmer until fork tender. In a large bowl, mash the potatoes as per your regular method, seasoning with rosemary, salt, pepper, adding milk or chicken or vegetable broth to have the right consistency (these are soft mashed potatoes that spread easily as a filling.)

When potatoes are boiling, start the caramelized onions. In a non-stick fry pan, heat the oil slightly and start slowly cooking the onion until they turn golden brown but do not crisp or dry out, about 20 minutes. Stir the caramelized onions into the mashed potatoes.

For the dough, using a food processor blend the water, lemon juice, eggs, salt, sugar, and oil and pulse to combine. Add flour and baking powder and process until a smooth mass forms. Add more flour as required. The dough should be smooth, elastic and slack. Remove from work bowl, cover with a damp tea towel and let rest one hour before using. Otherwise, place in a Ziploc bag, refrigerate until required (1-2 days) and allow to warm to room temperature before stretching.

Preheat oven to 350°.

Divide dough in two. On a lightly floured work surface, roll out each section to a 12 by 12 inch rectangle. Spread on half the mashed potatoes and press a chunk of cheese into the potatoes. Roll up into a log. Using a sharp knife or dough cutter, cut in 24-36 sections, depending on size you want. Turn cut side down and press slightly down, gather top cut edge inwards - to form a flower like opening or slight closure (almost as a rose is semi closed). For the egg wash, in a small bowl, whisk the eggs and oil together.

Stack two baking sheets together and line the top one with parchment paper. Place the knishes on the baking sheet. Brush the knishes all over with egg wash. Bake until golden brown, about 30-40 minutes.

These freeze well unbaked or baked. If baking frozen, just pop them in the preheated oven; you might need a few more minutes baking time.

Makes 24-35 small to medium knishes

Za'atar Smashed Potatoes

Olive oil, kosher salt and fresh and zesty za'atar transform spuds into an exotic event.

6-8 medium Yukon Gold or red-skinned potatoes

3 tablespoons olive oil

1/3 cup water

Juice of one lemon

¼ cup olive oil

½ teaspoon salt

¼ teaspoon pepper

6 cloves garlic, peeled

2 tablespoons za'atar spice

Preheat oven to 400°. Line a large baking sheet with parchment paper. Deeply score the potatoes and place on baking sheet. Drizzle on the water, lemon juice and olive oil. Season with the salt, pepper and scatter on the garlic. Then dust with the za'atar spice. Place in oven and reduce temperature to 375°. Bake until tender, about 40-50 minutes and then remove from oven and flatten potatoes with the back of a large spoon and return to oven, adding more salt, pepper to season to allow them to crisp up a bit on to.

Serves 4-6

Roasted Cauliflower with Kale and Sumac

Cauliflower has become popular lately, probably because of its versality. It's not quite a starch as a potato is, but it fits in this chapter because it is rustic and combined with kale (new) and sumac (old world) it's appetizing and perfect for so many occasions. For a variation, ditch the sumac for smoked Hungarian paprika or any spice you prefer.

Preheat oven to 375°. Line a baking sheet with parchment paper. Place kale on baking sheet, drizzle on the olive oil and dust with salt, pepper and sumac. Drizzle on lemon juice.

Bake until tender, 45 minutes.

Serves 6

1 bunch of kale, washed, spines removed

1 medium cauliflower, cored and trimmed

¼ cup olive oil

Salt, pepper, sumac

Juice of half a lemon

Kasha Varnishkes or Buckwheat and Bowties

You would be hard-pressed to find a more comforting recipe than this back-in-the-day comfort food of buckwheat groats, aka kasha, with bowtie pasta. This is the great peasant food of our forefathers. This is biblically grainy and on trend with healthy eating. Nice to see a legacy recipe getting its due!!

2 cups bowtie pasta, cooked

2 medium onions, finely minced

¼ cup vegetable oil

¾ cup buckwheat groats, medium or fine or a combo

1 egg

2 medium onions, finely chopped

2 cups bowtie pasta cooked

Salt, pepper

Water or chicken broth

(Start cooking the bowtie pasta according to package directions.)

Heat the onions in oil in a medium pan until almost golden brown, 10-15 minutes. Remove the onions.

In a medium bowl, mix the buckwheat and egg to coat the buckwheat. Heat the (same) pan over medium heat and stir in the buckwheat to toast it about four minutes. Add in ¼ teaspoon salt and a few pinches of black pepper. Remove from heat; add the onions.

Pour in the water or broth and stir; reduce heat and cover and let steam about 15 minutes. Fluff the buckwheat and turn out into a bowl. Toss with pasta and add a touch more oil if seems too dry and season with salt and pepper.

Serves 5-6

Caramelized Onions, Mushroom and Kale Kasha

This is a hearty dish that does well for fall holidays or a mid-winter Shabbat dinner. Dry roast the buckwheat in a skillet or purchase pre-toasted buckwheat. If you're not a fan of kale, swap in baby spinach.

Wash the buckwheat a few times and drain. Heat a medium skillet with one tablespoon of oil and over low-medium heat, toast the buckwheat five minutes. Remove from heat. Add the rest of the oil to the pan and slowly sauté the onions 5-10 minutes to soften and then add in mushrooms and cook until lightly browned, about 10-15 minutes. (If mixture sticks, add in a bit more oil). Add in the kale and cook briefly to soften.

In a 4-quart saucepan, heat the water to boiling. Add the salt and the toasted buckwheat and stir then cover and cook on lowest heat, for 20-30 minutes to soften the grain and the water evaporates. Stir in the onion, mushroom and kale and season with pepper, adding in more salt to taste.

Serves 4

1 cup medium buckwheat groats

3 tablespoons vegetable oil

1 medium onion, finely diced

2 cups mushrooms, washed and sliced

3 cups chopped kale, spines removed

2 cups water

½ teaspoon salt

¼ teaspoon pepper

Ginger Ale Glazed Sweet Potato Tzimmes

A glaze of ginger ale, cranberry and orange juices sweeten this Rosh Hashanah potato casserole, which can be assembled a day or two before. I prefer the addition of dried apricots and raisins, but dried prunes are traditional. Canned mandarin orange segments or cubed canned pineapple would also be a nice change. Although Tzimmes is typically served at Rosh Hashanah, it is welcome at any festive meal.

6-8 small sweet potatoes, about 3 pounds, peeled and quartered or halved

2 very large carrots, trimmed, scraped, and sliced in ¼ inch slices

Juice of one large orange

½ cup ginger ale

¼ cup apple or cranberry juice

¼ cup brown sugar

1/3 cup honey

½ cup sliced, dried apricots

¼ cup yellow raisins

3 tablespoons vegetable oil or unsalted margarine

Salt, pepper

Preheat the oven to 350°. Have a 6-quart oven casserole nearby, such as a rectangular roaster.

Prepare potatoes and carrots and place in roasting dish. Drizzle on the orange juice, ginger ale, apple juice, brown sugar, and honey. Add in the apricots, raisins and oil, season with salt and pepper and toss things around to let everything get coated with seasonings and liquid.

Cover and bake until potatoes are softened about 1 to 1½ hour, stirring occasionally. Remove cover for last 20 minutes of baking.

Serves 8-10

Rosh Hashanah Whipped Curried Apple Sweet Potatoes

Please don't ignore this recipe or pretend you assume you dislike curry because it's hot or too spicy. This is a spectacular dish that disappears the minute you serve it. It also features honey and apples making it a perfect side dish for your New Year's table, but this is welcome at any time. Any apples will work here but the orchard darling, i.e. Honey Crisp is especially recommended.

Boil the sweet potatoes until fork tender. Rinse and drain.

In a large bowl, mash the potatoes and then stir in the butter, honey and apples, and curry powder. Season with salt and pepper.

Serves 6-8

2 pounds peeled sweet potatoes (about 8 large potatoes)

½ cup unsalted butter, melted or vegetable oil

1/3 cup honey

2 cups shredded peeled apples

2-3 teaspoons curry powder, or to taste

Salt, pepper

Deli Style Potato Knishes

To me nothing beats a simple stretch dough as the easiest dough to work with and one that results in homey-tasting knishes that are good hot or cold. Huge ones are reminiscent of New York street vendor knishes, but small ones are more tender and crisp.

Stretch Knish Dough

¾ cup warm water

1 teaspoon fresh lemon juice

2 eggs

1 1/8 teaspoon salt

¼ teaspoon sugar

1/3 cup vegetable oil

3½ cups all-purpose flour

2 teaspoons baking powder

Mashed Potato Filling

4-6 cups mashed potatoes

1 large onion, very finely minced

3 tablespoons oil

Salt, pepper

Egg Wash

2 eggs

¼ cup vegetable oil

For the mashed potatoes, you will need about 2 pounds peeled potatoes to end up with 4-6 cups mashed potatoes. Peel the potatoes, place in a pot covered with water and bring to the boil. Simmer until fork tender. In a large bowl, mash the potatoes as per your regular method, seasoning with salt, pepper and adding milk (for a dairy meal) or chicken or warm vegetable broth (for a meat meal) to have the right consistency (these are soft mashed potatoes that spread easily as a filling.)

When potatoes are boiling, start the caramelized onions. In a non-stick fry pan, heat the oil slightly and start slowly cooking the onion until they turn golden brown but do not crisp or dry out, about 20 minutes.

For the dough, using a food processor or in a mixer bowl, blend the water, lemon juice, eggs, salt, sugar, and oil and pulse to combine. Add flour and baking powder and process until a smooth mass forms. Add more flour as required. Dough should be smooth, elastic and slack. Remove from work bowl, cover with a damp tea towel and let rest one hour before using. Otherwise, place in a Ziploc bag, refrigerate until required (1-2 days) and allow to warm to room temperature before stretching.

If making this in a stand mixer use the paddle attachment and add the water, lemon juice, eggs, salt and sugar to blend. Add flour and mix until mixture is a mass. Mix on slow speed, until dough is smooth and elastic, adding in only as much additional flour as required to make a soft dough. Cover and let rest 15-30 minutes (you can also wrap the dough and place in a lightly oiled Ziploc bag and refrigerate up to 2 days). Preheat oven to 350°.

Divide dough in two. On a lightly floured work surface, roll out each section to a 12x12 inch rectangle. Spread on half the mashed potatoes and roll up into a log. Using a sharp knife or dough cutter, cut in 15-20 sections. Turn cut side down and press slightly down, gather top cut edge inwards - to form a flower like opening or slight closure (almost as a rose is semi closed)

For the egg wash, in a small bowl, whisk the eggs and oil together.

Stack two baking sheets together and line the top one with parchment paper. Place the knishes on the baking sheet. Brush the knishes all over with egg wash. If you need more, whisk more eggs and oil together. Bake until golden brown, about 25-35 minutes.

Makes 24-35 small to medium knishes

New Way Hanukkah Potato Latkes

When my sons were little and enrolled in one Hebrew nursery school or another my kitchen was often the field trip for various Jewish holiday food excursions. One Hanukkah, forty toddlers ambushed my kitchen for a latke workshop. Clearly, I had to speed up production (toddlers aren't known to be patient) so my method was to par-boil the potatoes. Necessity is the mother of a new holiday invention and New Way Potato Latkes were the result. This new approach produced the best latkes ever. Ever. As far as latkes go, they break the mold and I promise you, once you make them this way, you'll never return to the traditional way. Doubt me? Make both styles, do a taste test and let me know how it goes!

6 medium-large red-skinned potatoes un-peeled

1 small onion, finely grated

3 eggs

2 tablespoons flour

1 teaspoon salt

¼ teaspoon pepper

Vegetable oil

Place potatoes in a medium saucepan and just cover with cold water. Turn heat to high and bring to a boil. As soon as potatoes are boiling, put a kitchen timer on for 10 minutes. When timer rings, remove potatoes from stove and cover with cold water. Drain immediately and cover immediately with very cold water. Let sit five minutes; then remove potatoes and pat dry.

Using a hand shredder (this is the best method) or food processor fitted with a medium disc, shred potatoes (with skins on; the skins will slide off anyway). The potatoes should be *slightly* softened, but still firm enough to produce shreds. Discard the peel as it separates from the potato but if some bits of peel get grated in with the potatoes, it's ok - just incorporate it into the mixture.

In a large bowl, blend shredded potatoes, eggs, grated onion, flour, salt, and pepper. Place newspaper on work surface (near frying area) and cover with a few paper towels. In a large deep skillet (a deep wok is perfect), pour in enough vegetable oil to reach two thirds up the side of the pan. If using an electric fry pan, set the temperature to 350° or 375°. (depending on how fast you want the pancakes to cook).

Drop potato batter by teaspoons (for small ones) or soup spoonfuls (larger ones), flattening slightly with a metal spatula if desired. I use large metal tongs for dropping and turning. Brown one side, turn once, and complete cooking on other side. These cook quickly. You're looking for a puffy centre while retaining some crisp shreds of potato on edges.

Serve immediately or freeze. To reheat, place latkes on a large wire cake rack on a cookie sheet and warm at 250° until crisp. For freezing purposes, fry them a little underdone to allow for browning in the re-heating stage.

Makes 3-3½ dozen, depending on size

Waffled Latkes

What happens when you take a unique potato pancake batter and deposit it on a waffle iron? Very newish-Jewish latkes! These are beautiful to look at, crisp and crunchy to eat and perfect for a Hanukkah gathering or to update a Shabbat supper. Try them with white potatoes but also a white and sweet potato combo or add some herbs. These would be lovely with a roasted apple slice on them or a dollop of Greek yogurt or artisanal sour cream.

3 medium large red-skinned or Yukon gold potatoes

2 tablespoons oil

2 tablespoons finely minced scallions

2 eggs

1 teaspoon salt

¼ teaspoon pepper

Vegetable oil

Place potatoes in a medium saucepan and just cover with cold water. Turn heat to high and allow to come to boil. As soon as potatoes are boiling, put a kitchen timer on for 7 minutes. When timer rings, remove potatoes from stove and cover with cold water. Drain immediately, and then cover again with cold water. Let sit five minutes. Remove potatoes and pat dry.

Using a hand shredder (best) or food processor fitted with a medium disc, shred potatoes (with skins on). The potatoes should be slightly softened, but still firm enough to produce shreds. If the peel separates from the potato, discard it. If the peel gets grated in with the potatoes, it's fine; incorporate into the mixture.

In a large bowl, blend shredded potatoes, grated onion, eggs, salt, and pepper.

Heat an electric waffle iron to medium-hot and drizzle with oil (top and bottom part).

Add 3-4 tablespoons potato batter to center of waffle iron, close top and cook about 3-4 minutes until waffles are crisp, brown and can be (using a fork), lifted in one piece off the grill.

Makes 12-20, depending on size

Traditional Potato Pancakes or Latkes

This is the easy and the classic recipe most families serve. It's a gold standard in its way and it has its place of honor but just try these against the New Way Latkes recipe in a taste test and see which ones you prefer!

In a food processor, dice up the onions and potatoes briefly. Add in eggs and process a bit more, and then remaining ingredients and process to make a batter, about 1-2 minutes.

Heat up some oil in a large skillet, about ½ inch up the sides. When the oil is hot, about 385°, drop dollops of the batter in the hot oil. Brown well on each side, turning once. Drain on paper towels.

Small latkes are crisper and cook (as well as disappear!) faster. Serve with sour cream and apple sauce on the side.

Makes 3 to 4 dozen, depending on size

4 medium potatoes, peeled and quartered

1 small onion peeled and quartered

2 eggs

1/3 cup flour

1 teaspoon baking powder

¾ teaspoon salt

¼ teaspoon pepper

Vegetable oil

New Way Sweet Potato Latkes

A new spin on my legendary New Way Potato Latkes but here sweet potatoes add vitamins and colour; the combination of gold and orange is simply beautiful.

3 medium to large Yukon gold potatoes (or any white potato)

3 medium sweet potatoes

1 small to medium onion, finely grated

2 eggs

1 teaspoon salt or to taste

¼ teaspoon pepper or to taste

Vegetable oil

Place potatoes in a medium saucepan and just cover with cold water. Turn heat to high and allow to come to boil. As soon as potatoes are boiling, put a kitchen timer on for 10 minutes. When timer rings, remove potatoes from stove and cover with cold water. Drain immediately, and then cover again with cold water. Let sit five minutes. Remove potatoes and pat dry.

Using a hand shredder (best) or food processor fitted with a medium disc, shred potatoes (with skins on). The potatoes should be slightly softened, but still firm enough to produce shreds. If the peel separates from the potato, discard it. If the peel gets grated in with the potatoes, it's fine and just incorporates it into the mixture. I like the hand grater best. When I use the processor, I use two thirds shredded then pulverized potatoes and one third shredded for a mixture than is bulky but still has shreds. Worth the trouble.

In a large bowl, blend shredded potatoes, grated onion, eggs, salt, and pepper. Place newspaper on work surface (near frying area) and cover with a few paper towels. In a large deep skillet (I like to use a wok), pour in enough vegetable oil to fill about two thirds. If using an electric fry pan, set the temperature to 350° or 375° (depending on how fast you want the pancakes to cook). Drop potato batter by teaspoons (for small ones) or soup spoonfuls in small dollops, flattening slightly with a metal spatula if desired.

Makes 3-4 dozen depending on size

Quick and Easy Potato Varenikes

Dumplings are trending but varenikes are forever. Dumplings (also similar to perogies) are what varenikes essentially are. Store-bought egg roll covers do the honors for homemade varenikes or you can also use the knish stretch dough or kreplach dough, both in this book. Kosher egg roll covers can be found in most supermarkets.

Prepare the mashed potatoes as per your preferred way to make mashed potatoes.

Fill a large pot with 8 cups of water and add 1 teaspoon salt and bring to a boil.

To assemble the varenikes, whisk an egg in a small bowl. Lay out some egg roll covers and brush the surface lightly with some egg wash. Deposit about a tablespoon of mashed potatoes a little over from the middle of each won ton square. Using a butter knife or ravioli cutter or stamp, press down to seal a packet or envelope.

Gently spoon dumplings into the water and simmer about 7-8 minutes until they are fully tender. Fry up in unsalted butter or serve with sour cream.

Makes 4-5 dozen

4 cups mashed potatoes

1 package egg roll covers, (use as many as required)

2 eggs

8 cups water

1 teaspoon salt

Butter or oil, for frying

Sour cream or Greek yogurt

Chapter Six
Kugels

Kugels

What is kugel? It's Yiddish and means 'pudding'. To me, kugel is anything but a pudding (unless you think of it like a baked rice pudding sort of way), it's more of a (usually) savory (or sometimes, sweet) casserole that has a noble tradition in the Jewish kitchen. When it comes to side dishes, kugel is a marquee player. Kugels are most likely made with noodles, or grated potatoes, carrots, matzoh meal and they can be sweet or savory. I never gave kugels much thought until I began making more diverse ones than the tried-and-true ones and that's how I broadened my repertoire and (kugel) respect. Hot and staying, warm or cold, they are as perfect alongside a brisket or roast chicken.

In addition to being versatile, kugels are universally easy, generally use pantry ingredients, freeze unbaked or baked or keep (refrigerated) for a few days. I've included the Jewish kitchens favorite, traditional kugels to start you off but also created a slew of exciting recipes that are nicely fresh and upbeat but still, as they say, 'kosher'. If you're planning a simple meal and want a change from potatoes or rice, kugels are your best bet! And don't forget there's more great kugels such as celebratory Three Level Kugel, Passover Matzoh Meal Kugel among others in the Passover Chapter.

New Year's Sweet Apple Raisin Kugel

A little extra sweetness is always welcome and especially at Rosh Hashanah. This is a gold standard, classic sweet kugel that hits those high notes for a happy New Year. A dairy version of this delectable sweet kugel follows.

Prepare noodles according to package directions and drain well. Let cool 10 minutes.

Preheat oven to 350°. Generously spray a 3-quart baking dish or square pan with non-stick cooking spray or smear with some oil.

In a large bowl, mix noodles with the oil, eggs, salt, sugar, honey, apples and raisins. Spoon into prepared baking dish. Drizzle top with a bit more oil. Dust top with sugar and cinnamon. Place on a parchment paper lined baking sheet. Bake until top is barely golden brown, about 35-45 minutes.

Serves 6-8

1 10-12 ounce package flat or broad egg noodles

¼ cup vegetable oil

4 eggs

1/8 teaspoon salt

1/3 cup sugar

2 tablespoons honey

2-3 cups chopped apples

½ cup raisins, plumped

Finishing Touches

Oil

Sugar

Cinnamon

Classic Dairy Sweet Kugel

A silken, smooth version of classic sweet kugel but with dairy overtones. I love adding apples or cranberries for Sukkot (as well as Thanksgiving) or Rosh Hashanah but you can also omit the fruit for a pure and simple sweet, dairy kugel.

1 10-12 ounce packages flat or broad egg noodles

¼ cup vegetable oil or unsalted butter

4 eggs

1/8 teaspoon salt

1/3 cup sugar

2 tablespoons honey

2 cups small curd cottage cheese

1½ cups sour cream or Greek yogurt

1½ teaspoons pure vanilla extract

2-3 cups apples, peeled and chopped

½ cup dried cranberries

Finishing Touches

Oil

Sugar

Cinnamon

Prepare noodles according to package directions, drain and let cool 10 minutes.

Preheat oven to 350°. Generously spray a 3-quart baking dish or square pan with non-stick cooking spray or smear with some oil.

In a large bowl, blend the noodles, oil, eggs, salt, sugar, honey, cottage cheese, sour cream, vanilla and apples. In a small bowl, add the cranberries and cover with steaming hot water for 2 minutes, drain and dry. Add the cranberries to the noodle mixer and spoon into prepared baking dish. Drizzle top with a bit more oil. Dust top with sugar and cinnamon. Place on a parchment paper lined baking sheet.

Bake until top is barely golden brown, about 35-45 minutes.

Serves 6-8

Spiralized Mini Potato Kugels

Spiralized potatoes make for exceptional kugel and these golden, crown-like kugels are good for the crown of the year (Rosh Hashanah) or Shabbat. If you don't have a spiralizer, use an inexpensive hand shredder easily found online. Similar to a potato or carrot peeler, a hand shredder makes nice strands of potatoes or you can also, if you have it, use the special shredding blade on your food processor.

Preheat oven to 400°. Generously brush the insides of silicone muffin cups with olive oil. In each, place (cut out to fit) a 'collar' of parchment paper to make a conical form. Brush inside of this collar with some olive oil. Line a baking sheet with parchment paper and place muffin pan on it.

Spiralize or otherwise shred the potatoes. Set aside. In a large bowl, mix the eggs, salt, pepper, onion powder, scallions and oil. Fold in the spiralized potatoes and mix very well to coat potatoes with other ingredients. Fill each muffin cup about half full of the potato mixture so that it's within ½ inch of the parchment paper collar.

Bake until crisped and brown, 45-55 minutes. Gently unmold kugels from the muffin mold and remove parchment paper collars to serve. Use a knife to separate sides if kugels stick.

Makes 12

Olive oil

6 medium potatoes, peeled

3 eggs

¾ teaspoon salt

½ teaspoon pepper

1 teaspoon onion powder

½ cup minced scallions or chives

½ cup vegetable oil

Butternut Squash, Pear and Apple Kugel

Naturally I think of this as a fall kugel for Sukkot or break-the-fast at Yom Kippur or anytime you want something a touch sweet and basking in autumn flavours. This is proof positive that kugel doesn't have to be potato or noodle based.

4 cups 1-inch cubed, peeled butternut squash (about 1½ pounds)

1 cup diced peeled apples

1 cup diced pears

2 eggs

½ cup all-purpose flour

¼ cup light brown sugar

2 teaspoons finely minced lemon zest

¼ cup maple syrup

1 teaspoon pure vanilla extract

½ teaspoon cinnamon

1/8 teaspoon allspice

1/8 teaspoon cloves

½ cup orange or apple juice

Preheat oven to 350°. Generously spray a 9-inch layer pan or 4-quart casserole with non-stick cooking spray. Line a baking sheet with parchment paper and place the oven dish on it.

Prepare the squash, apples and pears and place in a large bowl. Blend in the eggs, flour, brown sugar, lemon zest, maple syrup, vanilla extract, cinnamon, allspice, cloves and orange or apple juice and spoon into prepared dish.

Bake until tender, 55-60 minutes or until the top is golden brown and squash cubes are fork-tender. Let set a bit before serving.

Serves 6-8

Special Potato Onion Kugel-in-the-Round

A potato kugel is often a Passover side dish staple for Passover but it's welcome anytime. I bake this in a round pan for a prettier presentation and easier slicing and serving. It's wonderful served with brisket gravy.

Use a ring mold such as a non-stick tube or angel food cake pan. Spray very generously with non-stick cooking spray or smear with vegetable oil. Line inner sides and bottom with parchment paper. Place on a parchment paper-lined baking sheet.

Parboil potatoes first by putting them in a large pot and barely cover with cold water. Bring to a boil, reduce heat to low, and let simmer for 5 minutes. (Timing is everything for this recipe; it's really imperative in order to obtain best results) Remove and cover with cold water. Preheat oven to 350°.

Using a hand grater, shred potatoes. Put them in a large bowl and then toss with minced onions, parsley, salt, pepper, oil and eggs. Place in oven and bake until top is nicely browned, 35-45 minutes. Invert onto a platter before serving.

Serves 8-10

2½ pounds potatoes (about 7-8 medium large)

1 medium onion, finely minced

2 tablespoons parsley, finely minced

Salt, pepper

1/3 cup vegetable oil

4 eggs

Jerusalem Kugel

Although this incredible kugel calls for sugar it's not sweet! The sugar caramelizes and serves to make a crisp, beautifully bronzed outer layer. You can make this with egg noodles or even linguine noodles.

1 10-12 ounce package thin egg noodles or spaghetti, cooked

1 cup sugar

½ cup vegetable oil

6 eggs

1 teaspoon garlic powder

1 teaspoon onion powder

1½ teaspoons salt

½ teaspoon black pepper

Spray a 10-inch spring-form or angel food cake pan by spray with non-stick cooking spray. Place it on a parchment paper-lined baking sheet. Preheat oven to 350°.

In a 3-quart skillet, over medium heat, combine sugar and oil and over medium heat, for 10-15 minutes. Using a whisk, stir until the sugar dissolved and mixture begins to brown. (Oil and sugar might separate; it's fine). As soon as mixture seems bubbly or foamy (this takes about 20 minutes approximately) remove from stove and stir into the noodles. Let cool to almost room temperature and then blend in the eggs, garlic powder, onion powder, salt and pepper. Spoon into prepared baking dish and press down to even out top and make sure mixture is 'snug' in the pan.

Bake until top is crisped and browned, 60-65 minutes. Using knife to separate the noodles from the pan, unmold from the pan and turn out onto a serving platter.

Serves 8-10

Sundried Tomato Burrata Asiago Feta Kugel

This perky, sunny kugel is a dairy offering that is a sunny Mediterranean/ Yiddish cuisine mash-up that is totally memorable. You can swap Parmesan cheese for the Asiago if you prefer. This is perfect for Shavuot or a vegetarian Shabbat lunch or anytime you want a unique and zesty kugel.

Preheat oven to 350°. Prepare the noodles. Generously spray a 4-quart casserole with non-stick cooking spray. Line a baking sheet with parchment paper and place baking dish on it.

In a large bowl, mix the pasta with the olive oil, marinara sauce, tomato pesto, basil pesto, white wine, garlic, salt, pepper, oregano, basil, burrata, feta, Parmesan or Asiago cheese.

Spoon into prepared baking pan and bake until it sizzles, 40-45 minutes.

Serves 6-8

1 pound cooked pasta such as fettucine or short flat noodles

3 tablespoons olive oil

1½ cups marinara sauce

2 tablespoons sun-dried tomato pesto

2 tablespoons basil pesto

2 tablespoons white wine, optional

2 teaspoons finely minced garlic

½ teaspoon salt

¼ teaspoon pepper

1 teaspoon oregano

½ teaspoon basil

1 cup burrata, in small pieces

½ cup feta cheese, diced

½ cup Parmesan or Asiago cheese

Angel Hair Pasta Flowering Kugel

You can make a giant dish of this or many small ones. I like the small version since there's more crisp edges per capita —so to speak. Angel hair pasta works here or cappelletti or tangliatelle.

Olive oil

1 pound package cooked angel hair pasta

3 eggs

¾ teaspoon salt

½ teaspoon pepper

½ teaspoon onion powder

½ teaspoon garlic powder

½ cup finely minced green onion or chives

½ cup vegetable oil

Preheat oven to 425°. Generously brush the insides of muffin cups with olive oil. Line a baking sheet with parchment paper and place muffin tin on it.

Place the cooked pasta in a large bowl and mix with the eggs, salt, pepper, onion powder, garlic powder, green onion and oil. Place 1/3 cup of the mixture into muffin cups.

Bake until crisped and brown looking, 45-65 minutes. Use a knife to separate sides if kugels stick.

Makes 12

Potato Kugel or Miniature Kugel

This is one of my favorite ways to serve potato kugel because it features crispness on every surface. I enjoy these mini kugels alongside a hearty bowl of Russian Cabbage Soup. They're also perfect with a quick sweet-and-sour meatball supper.

Brush twenty-four muffin cups with vegetable oil. Place on a parchment paper line baking sheet.

Place potatoes in a medium saucepan and cover with cold water. Place pan on stovetop and turn heat to high. As soon as the water comes to a boil, set a kitchen timer for 10 minutes. When timer rings, drain potatoes and cover again with cold water.

Using a hand shredder (this is the best method) or food processor fitted with a medium disc, shred potatoes (with skins on; the skins will slide off anyway). The potatoes should be slightly softened, but still firm enough to produce shreds. Discard the peel as it separates from the potato. Preheat oven to 350°.

In a large bowl, blend shredded potatoes, eggs, onion, parsley, green onion, salt, pepper, onion powder and oil. Fill the muffin cups two-thirds full or a bit more with the batter.

Bake until crisped and sizzling, about 35-50 minutes, brushing with a bit of oil as they bake to help them crisp.

Makes 20-24, depending on size

6 medium potatoes

3 eggs

1 medium onion, finely grated

1 tablespoon minced parsley

3 tablespoons minced green onion

1 teaspoon salt

¼ teaspoon pepper

½ teaspoon onion powder

¼ cup vegetable oil

Primavera Rotini Kugel

Nothing is prettier than tri-colour rotini-shaped pasta when made into a kugel! If this is to be served with a dairy dish or fish, you can dust it with Parmesan cheese.

1 pound packaged tri-colour rotini pasta, cooked

3 eggs

¾ teaspoon salt

½ teaspoon pepper

1 teaspoon onion powder

1 teaspoon garlic powder

½ teaspoon oregano

¼ teaspoon basil

½ cup minced scallions

1/3 cup light olive oil

Preheat oven to 350°. Generously spray a 9-inch round baking pan with non-stick cooking spray.

Place the rotini pasta in large bowl and allow to cool to room temperature. When cool, mix with eggs, salt, pepper, onion powder, garlic powder, green onion, and oil.

Bake until crisp and brown 45-50 minutes. Cut into wedges and serve hot.

Serves 6-8

Sweet Potato Pie Kugel

———————————•·◆·•———————————

This is perfect almost anytime you want a slightly sweet kugel, especially at Sukkot or Yom Kippur but this is a fine one to choose anytime. If you want to serve this for Passover, use the matzoh meal and omit the baking powder and vanilla extract.

Preheat oven to 350°. Generously spray a 4-quart casserole dish with non-stick cooking spray or smear with oil.

Grate the sweet potatoes and apples and place in a large bowl. Blend in the orange juice, oil, eggs, vanilla, flour, baking powder, salt, cinnamon and pumpkin pie spice. Spoon mixture into the pan.

Bake until top is gently browned, 45 minutes. Let stand a bit before cutting.

Serves 6-8

6 medium sweet potatoes, peeled

1 medium apple, cored and peeled

3 tablespoons orange juice

¼ cup vegetable oil

3 eggs

1 teaspoon pure vanilla extract

1 cup flour or matzoh meal

½ teaspoon baking powder

¼ teaspoon salt

1 teaspoon cinnamon

½ teaspoon pumpkin pie spice

Cheddar Cheese Potato Yeasted Kugel

This is an outstanding and unique kugel or dinnertime side, for a dairy or parve supper. It bakes up puffy, crisp, and golden. Inside it is dense but not heavy, and streaked with melted cheese. Clearly this is for vegetarian, vegan or dairy dinner or even brunch, but it is certainly for cheese and potato lovers.

2 tablespoons oil

½ cup warm water

1 tablespoon instant yeast

1½ cups all-purpose flour

5-6 medium potatoes

1 medium onion, peeled

¼ teaspoon baking soda

1 teaspoon onion powder

1½ teaspoon salt

¼ teaspoon black pepper

2½ cup sharp cheddar cheese, grated

¼ cup vegetable oil

¼ unsalted butter, melted

3 eggs

Preheat oven to 350°. Drizzle the light olive oil in a 9-inch spring form layer pan or similar ovenproof casserole. Set aside.

In a mixing bowl, stir yeast into warm water and let sit a minute Stir in almost all the flour to make a thick batter, adding more flour, if required to achieve the right consistency. (If it is too thick to stir, drizzle in some more water). Cover and let stand 30 minutes.

Meanwhile, peel the potatoes and grate or shred them. Grate the onion.

When the batter has sat 30 minutes fold in the potatoes, onion, baking soda, onion powder, salt, black pepper, cheese, oil, butter and eggs. Mix well and then pour batter into prepared pan.

Place in oven, immediately lowering temperature to 325°; bake until nicely browned all over, about 50-60 minutes. Take out a small portion to see if it is baked through (potatoes will be cooked through).

Serve hot, warm, or cold.

Serves 8-10

Savory Sweet Potato Kugel

I love the color of this autumnal kugel which is good any time of year or for any of the Jewish holidays. Despite being made with sweet potatoes, this is a savory dish.

Preheat oven to 350°. Generously spray a 4-quart casserole dish with non-stick cooking spray or smear with oil.

Grate the sweet potatoes and place in a large bowl. Blend in the onion, scallions, olive oil, lemon juice, eggs, flour, bread crumbs, baking powder, salt, pepper and ginger. Spoon mixture into the pan.

Bake until top is gently browned, 45 minutes.

Serves 6-8

4 large sweet potatoes, peeled

1 medium onion, finely minced

4 scallions, finely diced

¼ cup light olive oil

2 tablespoons fresh lemon juice

4 eggs

¼ cup flour

¼ cup bread crumbs

¼ teaspoon baking powder

1½ teaspoons salt

¼ teaspoon pepper

1/8 teaspoon ginger

Traditional Noodle or Lokshen Kugel

Use flat egg noodles for this kugel. This is the serve-with-brisket or sweet and sour meatballs sort of kugel. It is never refused! In Yiddish, lokshen means noodles or pasta.

1 12 ounce package broad egg noodles

¼ cup vegetable oil

1 medium onion, coarsely chopped

5 eggs

Salt, pepper

Prepare noodles according to package directions and drain well.

Meanwhile, in a medium non-stick skillet, over medium or low heat, sauté the onions in the oil, gently, until golden.

Preheat oven to 350°. Generously spray a 9-inch baking dish with non-stick cooking spray or smear with some oil. In a bowl, mix the noodles with the onions, eggs, salt and pepper and then spoon into prepared baking dish.

Bake until lightly golden brown, about 35-45 minutes.

Serves 6-8

Carrot Cake Kugel

This is a classic carrot cake flavor in a kugel spin. Get ready to enjoy a sweet kugel with the light touch of spice.

First, cook the carrots by simmering in water until tender. Drain, cool and finely chop the carrots.

Preheat the oven to 350°. Generously spray a 4-quart casserole or oven proof dish with non-stick cooking spray.

In a large bowl, blend the carrots, eggs, oil, sugar, apple, raisins, cinnamon, orange juice, lemon juice, vanilla, cinnamon, salt, flour and baking powder. Spoon into prepared casserole.

Bake until set, about 35 minutes (it might puff and fall a bit; that's fine). Cut into squares to serve.

Serves 6-8

3 cups carrots, in chunks

4 eggs

¼ cup vegetable oil

½ cup sugar

1 apple, cored, peeled and grated

½ cup raisins, coarsely chopped

½ teaspoon cinnamon

2 tablespoons fresh orange juice

1 tablespoon fresh lemon juice

2 teaspoons pure vanilla extract

1 teaspoon cinnamon

¼ teaspoon salt

1/3 cup flour

1 teaspoon baking powder

Hanukkah Mac and Cheese Mini Kugels

Baked in muffin cups, this creamy, irresistibly cheesy Mac and Cheese bakes up into a perfect snack food, that is great for kids, especially during Shavuot or another dairy-based holiday or for a non-meat Saturday lunch.

2 cups elbow macaroni, cooked

Melted butter, for brushing pan

3 tablespoons unsalted butter

3 tablespoons flour

1¼ cups milk

2½ cups medium orange Cheddar cheese, shredded

1 cup Havarti or Monterey Jack cheese, shredded

1 teaspoon dry mustard

Salt, pepper

¼ teaspoon paprika

1/8 teaspoon cayenne

2 eggs

Soda Cracker Crumb Topping

1¼ cups crushed soda crackers

1/3 cup butter, melted

Salt, pepper

Preheat oven to 350°. Brush 18 muffin cups with some melted butter and place on a baking sheet.

In a 4-quart saucepan, melt the butter and add the flour and cook to brown flour slightly. Slowly pour in the milk and let warm very briefly, and then add in the cheeses, and seasonings. Cook over low heat to melt the cheeses so you have a nice saucy mixture. Let cool 20 minutes or until room temperature and stir in the eggs. Then stir the macaroni into the sauce. Using an ice-cream scoop, spoon mixture into the prepared muffin tins filling them quite full.

Meanwhile, in a small bowl, mix the soda cracker crumbs, butter, salt and pepper. Sprinkle a small amount over each 'muffin'.

Bake until set, 35-45 minutes until the cheese is bubbling. Allow the muffins to cool to set up the cheese and make them easier to handle, about 30 minutes.

Makes about 18, depending on size

Chapter Seven
Chicken and Turkey

Chicken and Turkey

Like the comforts of a great soup, nothing reaches into your tummy's soul like a great chicken dish. On its own chicken lends itself to a variety of flavours and spice approaches as well as cooking methods. But in the Jewish kitchen, chicken is pretty much hallowed fare; modest but certainly hallowed. A great Friday night roast chicken might be simple but along with the challah, makes the meal a feast. It is so indelible and traditional that just putting it out on the table is shorthand for Shabbat Shalom.

Of course, Friday Night Chicken (which is the name of one of my own favorite recipes I often make for my family) is just the beginning of a chicken (and turkey) repertoire that I am ever adding to.

Since chicken is so adaptable to so many approaches, I often use it, meal-wise speaking, as the foundational 'ingredient' to a cuisine I might want to try. I might not want the whole meal to be Sephardic/Moroccan or Hungarian Jewish, but the chicken, even as it is the meal's main event, is perfect to do my experimenting with. That being the case, I am delighted to share chicken recipes that are a wide gamut of updated East Euro classics, deli/grandma retro favs and Middle Eastern spins. Some recipes and renditions are what I call everyday dishes that you'll want to repeat a few times a month. Others are uniquely appropriate to a particular Jewish holiday.

What you need to know about chicken is to stock up since there's so many approaches that work with this basic protein. Other than that, be open to new flavours, always use fresh spices and herbs as well as kosher salt and pungent, fragrant pepper. Remember to have fresh parsley on hand as well as lots of garlic, piquant lemons and some white wine. The rest, as they say, will take care of itself. Don't forget, there are also some other great chicken dishes in the Passover chapter.

My Favourite Friday Night Spice and Lemon Roast Chicken

◆

This is chicken with a reputation. At least, it's made my reputation. The trick is to be generous with the spices and use the pickled lemons called for (but regular lemons are fine). The result is a spice crusted, lemon garlic chicken that is my go-to roast chicken for Friday nights, no matter what season. Saturating the skin with spices makes it crisp and reduces basting. Make sure you use coarse kosher salt - not regular salt. Superb hot or cold, this recipe is so good that I usually bake three small chickens which fly the coop fast. It ensures there's plenty of flavorful, seasoned chicken for chicken sandwiches the next day on a fresh slab of challah.

* You can also use *salted lemons* as per the recipe for Middle Eastern Salted Lemons that follows

Preheat oven to 375°.

Place chicken in roasting pan. Rub chicken with olive oil and squeeze lemons over and then stuff lemons remnants into cavity along with the onion. Add water, wine, parsley, rosemary and scatter garlic cloves around chicken. Completely coat chicken with all remaining spices except the salt. You should not be able to see any skin as chicken should be totally coated in spices. Sprinkle on salt.

Roast chicken about 1½ hours, basting with pan juices just a few times but for the last third of cooking, let the chicken roast without basting and also lower oven temperature to 350°. Cover any exposed skin with additional garlic and paprika that comes off as you baste.

Remove or squeeze the softened garlic (in the pan), discard papery exteriors and mash up the baked garlic into the roasting pan juices which can be used as a side gravy for the chicken.

Serves 4-5

1 3-4 pound chicken

2 tablespoon light olive oil

2 large lemons, quartered *

1 onion, quartered

½ cup water

¼ cup white wine

12 large garlic cloves, not peeled

¼ cup parsley, coarsely chopped

1 tablespoon fresh rosemary

2 tablespoons garlic powder

2 tablespoons paprika

1 pinch sage or poultry seasoning

1 pinch celery seed powder

½ teaspoon cumin

1 - 2 teaspoons coarse salt

Middle Eastern Salted Lemons

I always have a jar of these on hand in the fridge. Salted lemons are made in five minutes and they get better as they marinate and age. I use them in chicken dishes or minced up in grainy salads. The juice of salted lemons makes broiled fish sing with flavor!

Juice from 6 large lemons

6 whole lemons, washed

Coarse sea salt (very coarse crystals)

Black peppercorns

½ teaspoon chili pepper, optional

Quarter lemons vertically from top to within ½ inch of bottoms (do not cut all the way through). Sprinkle salt (¼ to ½ teaspoon) on exposed fruit and close lemon. Place 1 tablespoon of salt on the bottom of a large Mason jar. Squish a lemon or two into the jar, add a few teaspoons of salt on top and then add more lemons, squishing down (releasing some juice and packing jar as snugly as you can with lemons) and salting as you pack the jar with lemons. As you add the salt, add some peppercorns (and chili pepper if you're using it).

Cover with lemon juice and seal. Let stand in a warm area for at least 30 days, turning jar upside down each day to distribute salt and juices. If a cloudy growth appears, remove it with a wooden spoon.

These keep 1-2 months refrigerated.

Balsamic Roast Chicken

What's more elegant and downright delicious than this dish? It's a breeze to whip up and it's suitable for Passover or the High Holidays Since this is roasted in parts, versus whole chicken, it makes Passover serving really easy.

Preheat the oven to 350°. In a small bowl, mix the rosemary, thyme, parsley and garlic together. Loosen skin of chicken and place a little bit of the mixture underneath the skin.

Place the onions on the bottom of a roasting pan, then the mushrooms, leeks and carrots. Place chicken pieces on top. Mix wine and vinegar together and pour over chicken. Dust chicken generously with salt and pepper and drizzle on the olive oil.

Cover gently with foil and roast 1½-2 hours until chicken is tender. Remove foil, baste chicken and let brown another 15 minutes. (If pan juices evaporate, add a bit of water or chicken broth to ensure pan juices don't dry out.)

Serves 4-5

1 3-4 pound chicken, cut-up

2 teaspoons rosemary

2 teaspoons thyme

2 tablespoons finely minced parsley

3 garlic cloves, finely minced

2 medium red onions, sliced

1 cup small mushrooms

1 cup sliced leeks

1 cup sliced carrots

½ cup dry red wine

½ cup balsamic vinegar

Salt, pepper

1-2 tablespoons extra virgin olive oil

Chicken Sofrito

A classic dish, traced back to Spanish Jews, this zesty all-in-one chicken, potatoes and seasoned rice casserole is sunny as can be with vibrant turmeric, paprika, and other good things. It befits any occasion but it is especially welcome for the fall High Holidays, Sukkot and Tu Bishvat.

3-4 pounds chicken breasts and thighs, cut-up

Flour, salt, pepper

2 tablespoons light olive oil

3 garlic cloves, minced

½ cup finely minced onion

1 tablespoon paprika or smoked paprika

1 2 teaspoon chili powder

1¼ teaspoon turmeric

1 teaspoon garlic powder

¼ teaspoon cayenne

¼ teaspoon thyme

1 14 ounce can chopped tomatoes

2 cups chicken stock

¼ cup white wine

4 medium potatoes, halved

1 cup rice

Parsley, minced

Preheat oven to 350°.

Generously dredge the chicken pieces with salt and pepper. In a large roasting pan warm up the oil on the stovetop and place skin-side down in the oil, browning on both sides, turning once, about 7-10 minutes. Remove chicken.

To the roasting pan, add the garlic, onion, paprika, chili powder, turmeric, garlic, cayenne, and thyme and cook brief to soften the garlic about 5 minutes. Add in the tomatoes, chicken stock, wine, potatoes and white rice and stir briefly. Add in the chicken pieces. Cover and bake until done, 40-50 minutes. Adjust salt and pepper.

Serves 4

Apples and Honey Chicken

This lovely chicken dish is creamy (coconut milk or almond milk) and vibrant with apples and honey to celebrate Rosh Hashanah or any holiday

Dust the chicken pieces with flour and season with salt and pepper. Heat the oil in a Dutch oven and add the chicken pieces and sauté the chicken over medium low heat to brown the chicken turning once, about 5-8 minutes per side. Drain on paper towels and keep aside while preparing the rest of the recipe. Drain most of fat out of Dutch oven.

Sauté the minced shallot onion in the (same) Dutch oven. Then add garlic and about 2 tablespoons of flour. Stir to cook shallot and brown the flour, about 2-3 minutes. Then pour on the chicken broth and simmer 1-3 minutes to allow broth to thicken.

Place the chicken in the broth in the Dutch oven. Scatter the apples on top and drizzle on the apple cider and honey over chicken.

Cover and place in oven, reducing heat to 350°. Bake about 30 minutes, and then reduce heat to 325°. Pour on coconut if using, give things a stir and allow to finish cooking another 15 minutes, without cover on and sauce will thicken a bit more as it cooks down.

Serves 3-4

2 chicken breasts, cut in two pieces each

2 leg and thigh pieces, cut at the joint

Flour, salt, pepper

2-3 tablespoons light olive or vegetable oil

1 large shallot or onion minced

1 small clove garlic, minced

2 tablespoons flour

1 cup chicken broth

4 large apples pared, cored, cut in wedges

1½ cups apple cider or juice

¼ cup honey

¼ cup coconut or almond milk, optional

Preheat oven to 375°.

Cumin Sesame Roast Chickpea Chicken Bowls

<hr>

Bowl-food comes to the newish Jewish kitchen! I love bowl food especially
when it features some of my favorite ingredients and also has a healthy vibe.
You can triple the recipe and make this a buffet dish for Sukkot.

Bowl Food Part

1 pound skinless chicken breast

1 cup chick peas

1 cup cooked couscous or
quinoa, cooked

1 cup fresh corn

Marinade

1 tablespoon fresh lemon juice

1 tablespoon honey

1 tablespoon tahini

½ teaspoon garlic powder

1/8 teaspoon cumin

1/8 teaspoon coriander

¼ teaspoon salt

1/8 teaspoon pepper

1 scallion, finely minced

Finishing Touches

Lettuce greens

Sesame seeds

Sumac

Cilantro, minced

Pomegranate seeds

Cut the chicken breasts in large strips. In a medium bowl, mix the lemon juice, honey, tahini, garlic, cumin, coriander, salt, black pepper and onion. Toss in the chicken and marinate 30 minutes in the fridge or overnight. Have the other ingredients ready to go (prepared couscous or quinoa, canned corn)

Preheat oven to 375°. Line a baking sheet with parchment paper. Place the chicken on the sheet and bake until done, about 25-30 minutes. Remove and slice into small chunks or strips.

Prepare a bowl by placing some lettuce greens in the bowl, add some couscous in bowl, then the chick peas and top with the chicken strips. Drizzle on Lemon Sumac Vinaigrette and dust with sesame seeds, sumac, cilantro and pomegranate seeds.

Serves 1-2

Lemon Sumac Vinaigrette

The perfect salad dressing for Cumin Sesame Bowl Food or any green salad.

In food processor, blend all ingredients except the oils for two minutes. Put three types of oil in a 2-cup measuring cup. Very slowly drizzle in oil as mixture blends and thickens, 2-3 minutes.

Makes 1¼ cup

2 tablespoons minced garlic

2 tablespoons tahini

3 tablespoons fresh lemon juice

1 tablespoon wine vinegar

1 teaspoon honey

¾ teaspoon salt

¼ teaspoon pepper

¼ teaspoon dried chili flakes

1 teaspoon cumin

½ teaspoon coriander

½ teaspoon onion powder

½ teaspoon garlic powder

½ teaspoon sumac

1 tablespoon sesame seeds

¼ cup extra virgin olive oil

½ cup light olive oil

½ cup vegetable oil

Lemon, Artichoke and Olives Skillet Chicken

This is a spin on a classic lemony dish made all in one cast iron skillet. The artichokes and olives bring an ageless Middle East vibe, making this at home in the Jewish kitchen for almost any occasion. I think it's perfect for Shabbat.

1 3-4 pound chicken, split, backbone removed

2 teaspoons fresh thyme leaves

2 teaspoons salt

¾ teaspoon pepper

1/3 cup olive oil

1 lemon washed and sliced

1 large onion sliced

4 garlic cloves, peeled and sliced

½ cup dry white wine

1 10-12 ounce canned drained artichoke hearts

½ cup pitted Nicoise olives

Juice of one lemon

Preheat oven to 450°. Prepare the chicken by splitting in half and removing back bone.

In a small bowl, mix the thyme, salt, pepper and olive oil. Place the lemons, onion and garlic on the bottom of a 12-inch cast iron skillet. Place the chicken, skin side down on top. Smear the oil herb mixture all over the chicken.

Roast the chicken for 30 minutes and then pour the wine in the pan, around the chicken. Add in the olives and artichokes. Roast another 10-20 minutes until the chicken tests done (155-160°) and is nicely browned all over. Remove the chicken from the oven and drizzle on the lemon juice.

Serves 4

Spicy Moroccan Chicken

This is a slightly more exotic ciq au vin that totally perks up the palate. If you have preserved, salted lemons, that's ideal but if not, fresh, thinly sliced lemons are fine. A crock pot or other slow cooker is perfect for this. This is spicy and satisfying and a big platter of lemony couscous such as Royal Couscous (in index) goes perfect with it.

Preheat oven to 350°.

In a 5-6 quart Dutch oven casserole, heat the oil and add the chicken pieces, dusting generously with salt and pepper. Lightly brown the chicken and then add in the onions and sauté to soften, about 15 minutes and then add in the garlic and cook another 5 minutes (do not brown the garlic).

Add in the olives, lemons, fennel seeds, turmeric, cumin, chilli flakes, cinnamon, chicken broth and white wine. Place Dutch oven in the oven, reduce the temperature to 325° and cook until chicken is tender about two hours. Keep warm until serving. To serve, garnish with minced cilantro.

Serves 4-5

1 3-4 pound chicken, cut in 8ths

Salt, pepper

3 tablespoons olive oil

1 large onion, finely sliced

8 large garlic cloves, finely minced

1 cup pitted green olives

2 large lemons washed, thinly sliced

½ teaspoon fennel seeds

2 teaspoons turmeric

1 teaspoon cumin

1 teaspoon chilli flakes

½ teaspoon cinnamon

3 cups chicken broth

1/3 cup white wine

3-4 tablespoons minced cilantro

Vintage Style Bar Mitzvah Chicken

Vintage style roast chicken, aka Grandma-style chicken always has an extra homey flavor, the result of the generous use of the Jewish triumvirate spice combo of onion powder, garlic powder and paprika. Add some onions, mushrooms, rosemary and a bit of wine and you have a taste of the 1950s with a new millennium upgrade. Totally retro but delicious.

1 4-5 pound chicken, cut up

2 cups sliced mushrooms

1 cup sliced onions

1½ cups baby carrots

6 garlic cloves, peeled

½ cup water or chicken broth

¼ cup white wine

Salt, pepper

1 tablespoon onion powder

1 tablespoon garlic powder

2 tablespoons paprika

¼ teaspoon thyme

½ teaspoon rosemary

2 tablespoons finely minced parsley

Preheat oven to 350°. In a 4-5 quart roasting casserole, place the chicken and cover with the mushrooms, onions, and garlic. Put water and wine around sides. Add carrots around the sides. Drizzle oil on chicken pieces and then dust with salt, pepper, onion powder, garlic powder, paprika, thyme, rosemary and parsley.

Bake until tender 50-60 minutes, lightly covered and then uncover. Continue cooking 20-30 minutes longer, basting often and adding more broth or water if needed to make enough pan roasting gravy so chicken doesn't dry out.

Serves 5-6

Sephardic Spiced Chicken Cholent

This is more usually done with beef but for a change, I created a Sephardic-spiced chicken cholent which slow cooks in the oven for a beautiful, soulful dish. I love this for Sukkot or for a Shabbat lunch, of course, for which cholents were intended.

Preheat oven to 325°. In a small bowl, soak the saffron threads in two tablespoons of hot water.

Dust the chicken generously with salt and pepper. Heat up the oil in the pan and add the chicken pieces and brown on each side, 10-15 minutes. Remove from the pan and set aside. Add the onions, garlic and cook over medium heat to soften. Add in the soaked saffron, chick peas, sweet potatoes, white potato, rice, turmeric, cinnamon, allspice, paprika, cumin and honey. Add the chicken and stir and then add enough chicken stock or water to just cover chicken. Gently lower in eggs. Cover and place in oven and cook until done, 2½ - 3 hours.

Serves 4-5

¼ teaspoon saffron threads

3 pounds chicken parts (legs and breasts)

Salt, pepper

3 tablespoons olive oil

2 medium onions, chopped

6 cloves garlic, finely minced

2 15-ounce cans chick peas

2 large sweet potatoes, peeled and cut into large chunks

1 large white potato, cut into large chunks

1 cup rice

¾ teaspoon turmeric

½ teaspoon cinnamon

1 teaspoon allspice

1 tablespoon paprika

2 teaspoons cumin

1 tablespoon honey

4-6 eggs (in shell)

Chicken stock or water

Mint

Sticky Pomegranate Chicken

Ah, the flavors of the bible, as expressed with honey and pomegranate. What's more satisfying than a unique spin on 'stickie chickie' than this recipe! for legs but you can also use chicken breasts, cut in quarters for this delicious dish.

¼ cup pomegranate molasses or balsamic vinegar

2 tablespoons light olive oil

2 tablespoons tomato paste

1 tablespoon honey

½ teaspoon cinnamon

3 pounds chicken legs

2 red onions

1/3 cup pomegranate spirals

Cilantro, minced

In a medium bowl, mix the pomegranate molasses with the oil, tomato paste, honey and cinnamon. Add the chicken onions and marinate in the fridge 30 minutes or overnight.

Preheat oven to 350°. Line a baking sheet or roasting pan with foil. Place the chicken pieces on it and bake 35-45 minutes until chicken is cooked through. Transfer to a serving dish and spoon pan juices over chicken. Garnish with minced cilantro and scatter on pomegranate seeds on top. Rice or potatoes dusted with sumac is a nice side dish.

Serves 4

Brined Hanukkah Roast Turkey

Brining turkeys is a trend that's staying and also works with kosher turkey. Just avoid using pre-basted turkey. Hannukah is the festive occasion I'd choose to serve this glorious turkey, alongside platters of potato latkes and bowls of apple sauce. Your own favorite stuffing works here or you can opt for the Matzoh Stuffing in the Passover chapter, swapping in bread cubes for the matzoh.

Brined Turkey

1 10-14 pound turkey, not pre-basted

2 cups table salt

¼ cup sugar

Water to cover turkey

Pan Stuff

2 carrots cut up

2 ribs celery, cut up

2 cups water

½ cup white wine or water

½ cup chicken bouillon

1 lemon, quartered

1 medium onion, peeled and quartered

Herb Slather

1 cup fresh parsley, finely chopped

2 tablespoons fresh rosemary

2 tablespoons fresh sage

4 sprigs crumbled fresh thyme

2 scallions diced

Zest of one lemon

3 large cloves garlic, peeled

6 tablespoons light olive oil

2 teaspoons salt

1 teaspoon pepper

Roasting Pan Extras

¼ cup olive oil or melted margarine

Salt, pepper, Bell's Seasoning or dry sage, paprika, garlic powder

In a 12-quart stockpot, one that is big enough to fit the turkey, stir the salt, sugar and water together to dissolve the salt and sugar. Place the turkey inside and allow to sit in the brine, in a cool place (garage under 50°, or fridge) for 4 hours. Drain and pat dry; discard the brine.

Preheat the oven to 400° and place the turkey in the roasting pan. Add in entire 'pan stuff' to the pan.

For the Herb Slather, add all ingredients, except the spices to be used to dust the outside of the turkey, to a food processor. Process to make the herbs into a paste. Lifting the skin of the turkey from the area where the cavity is (where you usually put the stuffing), using your fingertips spread equal amounts of the Herb Slather on the breast area of both sides of the turkey as evenly as you can. Pat the skin down gently.

Place the turkey in the roasting pan. Brush the turkey with olive oil or margarine and then dust with some salt, pepper, the Bell's Seasoning or sage, paprika and garlic powder.

Roast turkey for at least 1½ hours and then reduce the temperature to 350°, basting 3-4 times during overall roasting. You need allow for 20 minutes per pound, or 3½ to 5 hours, depending on size of the bird. Use an oven thermometer to ensure it is evenly cooked through and is 180-185°.

Don't baste turkey within about 30 minutes of it being done, to allow skin to crisp. If pan juices evaporate, add ½ cup water or more, as required to pan bottom. Use juices that remain to make gravy. Let turkey stand about 15-20 minutes before carving.

Serves 10-12

Chapter Eight
Beef (Mostly Briskets and

Meatballs)

Beef (Mostly Briskets and Meatballs)

For a long time, it seems that 'meat' aka, old-fashioned meat and potato repasts, hasn't been fashionable, unless you're a weekend BBQ warrior or the proud owner of a Memphis smokehouse. As a 'lunch-time vegetarian' I can appreciate that, because I tend to eat light and beef doesn't always figure in 'lite'. But once in while I admit that nothing is as satisfying as meat and potatoes. To be more precise, what is better than a succulent, well-cooked brisket, cooked in oh-so-many ways? Brisket and mashed potatoes, brisket and knishes or smashed, garlic potatoes or brisket and latkes? How good is that? Let me count the ways! I guess to some extent when we think of 'meat' in the Jewish kitchen, we're thinking: brisket. No other cuisine seems to make such a fuss over it or be as competitive, for that matter. I grew up hearing about legendary 'great brisket' makers and my mother-in-law was one of the best brisket makers I know. I myself make a new brisket recipe every other month – for those times that nothing else but 'meat' will do.

Brisket comes in two cuts: first or second cut. Whereas 'first cut' sounds better and is less fatty (which you would think is a good thing) second cut brisket is tastier, moister and the one I'd recommend. It cooks better with that bit of fat, which you can always trim a bit off before or after cooking.

Sinewy and therefore needing some TLC, brisket is traditionally cooked long and slow. Then it rests in the fridge overnight and hours before serving, it is customarily sliced then, arranged in its roasting pan juices and enjoys a slow, second roast to tenderize the meat and further infuse it with flavor. I spent years making brisket this way and now I have two more approaches. Approach one is: slow cook it so long and slow that it has no choice but to tenderize itself and get imbided with flavor. Approach two is: use a slow cooker, pressure cooker, crock pot or Instapot which makes short of brisket and ensures it's fork-tender. My only caveat with the second approach is that it takes a bit of finessing to figure out, depending on which cooking vehicle (pressure cooker, crock pot, Instapot, etc.) you're using. You need to record how much liquid is necessary for alternate cooking vessels (whereas in a regular roasting pan, I tend to know what works) and how much time (and at what temperature or cycle) is required. I find that (to be honest) a bit of a pain. So, find the cooking pot that suits your needs, lifestyle, and timing and stick with it. Then you won't have to readjust recipes. Much like cooking with convection or traditional heat sources, you just need to be a bit more meticulous so as not to have surprises like dried up meat in a stock-free pot or not enough spice or mushy meat or tough meat – simply because it was missing one small element. As I said, there's the finessing issue when cooking brisket in alternate cooking vessels.

Of course, there's more than brisket in the Jewish (beef) kitchen. There's Beef Short Ribs, my mother-law Shirley's famed Garlic Cross Rib Roast and of course, our national treasure: Sweet and Sour Meatballs.

The Details on Brisket

When it comes to brisket, I've often quipped that whereas people were always asking me for yet another stellar cheesecake, no one ever beat a path to my door imploring me for a better brisket recipe. It got chuckles, but it is, as it happens, also untrue. People always do seem on the look-out for bigger and more unique (and still easier to prepare) brisket as much as they are sniffing around for a better poppy seed cookie or flakier rugulah. I am pleased to get asked often for my brisket recipes (from those who've had holiday meals here and had one or another of the briskets from my repertoire). Indeed, every holiday seems to set me on a new brisket trail. Being as it is the holiday centerpiece, I am always inspired by new possibilities. In the Jewish holiday kitchen, a person's prowess at making a great brisket can make them a family legend. It is where one's ability as a flavor maven truly shines.

We all have a few recipes from our mothers, to grandmothers, friends and aunts and Ida's second-cousin's aunt's sister-in-law's brisket. And we alternate – making the tried and true with looking for one new one that tastes different or better. Ironically, one of the best, albeit dubious compliments you can receive is that 'your brisket doesn't taste like…. brisket' (which is, in savory terms, is on a par with the phrase that 'your Passover cake doesn't taste like a Passover cake'. I'm not in total agreement with the back-handed brisket compliment but I concede, all things being equal, a different brisket recipe is both fun and flavorful. Holiday times are just the occasions to decant a new one and see if you have found a new treasure.

In the traditional Jewish kitchen, brisket means: holidays. At the least, it signifies Shabbat. Elsewhere, like Texas, brisket crosses over into barbecue food and people start talking about pits and rubs, but to kosher cuisine, brisket means love and home (and holidays). An unusual meat, brisket would be tough and sinewy if you roasted it dry and ate it soon after it was done. But let it do a lazy braise in delectable gravy and you have a totally different dish.

As varied as brisket recipes might be, there are things all briskets have in common, so check out my Brisket Basics List.

Brisket Basics

What cut of meat is a brisket exactly?

A brisket is a boneless roast that comes from the front quarters of a steer. You do not have to be Jewish nor kosher to enjoy brisket – it is simply a specific cut of beef, but if you have trouble finding one in your regular supermarket, try a kosher butcher. Small roasts may seem tempting or be more economical but larger ones roast better. Besides which, brisket is the sort of thing you want to have leftovers of for another hot roast beef meal or for incredible brisket sandwiches. This is one cut of meat that is as good cold as it is hot. So, look for a 5-6 pound brisket (and cooked leftovers, incidentally, also freeze well).

Brisket comes labelled as either first or second cut. Second cut makes a better, though somewhat fattier, roast. First cut is far leaner which is gentle on calories, but the fattier meat does better in the long braise brisket calls for. You can also, once the meat is chilled, trim off the fat and skim additional fat that has formed in the gravy. If there is obvious fat on the raw brisket, you can certainly trim this off before cooking, although some fat helps the meat cook with added flavor, moistness and tenderness.

Brisket is a rather sinewy roast, suited to long braising, tons of flavorings (dry rubs, marinades et al) and is traditionally slow roasted or braised, cooled, then sliced, and re-braised in its pan juices, rendering lean and tender portions for serving at a sit-down meal. But some of my brisket recipes call for an even longer roasting in a very slow oven (300°). You'll find this method yields mouth-wateringly tender brisket without necessity for a second slice, warm and braise method, most brisket recipes call for. Because brisket has a definite grain, it must be cut 'across the grain' to result in tender slices (rather than sinewy ones).

Foil the Roasting Pan!

Brisket makes for hard-to-clean roasting pans. It is a good idea to fully line bottom of pan with heavy duty foil wrap to make clean-up (and catching all those pan juices) easier or use a non-stick roaster.

A Note on Cholents

Most cultures have an all-in-one slow cooking meal but cholent, a Shabbat staple, has a sacred spot on the Jewish menu – especially in times past, when a little meat and a lot of beans had to go a long way. Slow braising tenderizes lean cuts of meat, but it also is the epitome of a make-ahead main dish. A nice-sized crock pot would be perfect for this traditional all-in-one meal, but I slow bake in a heavy casserole (such as Le Creuset) it in a low temperature oven. Observant families might keep their cholent on a low burner covered with aluminum sheeting, and let it cook itself to hearty perfection, with barely a stir – just hot and perfectly in time for a Shabbat luncheon. Cholent would be perfect pre or post Yom Kippur meal. No matter when you serve this, it is heartwarming, memorable food and nutritious. Cholent recipes are incredibly varied; kosher community cookbooks featured almost as many cholents as honey cakes and challah recipes! There are cholents with chicken or vegetarian approaches. You can experiment with different grains and legumes (couscous or quinoa, rice, or other beans), as well as the spices, which would dramatically alter the final flavor (curry or cumin, vs. the garlic, onion and paprika route). This cholent is an easy, wonderfully classic one to start with. The scent of it cooking is as homey and old school as you please, and it offers nostalgia and nutrition in every delectable spoon or forkful.

Cholent in Crock Pot, Pressure Cooker or Instapot

When making any main dish, especially beef (or chicken), you must adapt your recipe to the appliance or cooking vessel. It takes a bit of finessing. So, take notes (adding in more water or less stock, adjust spice or the timing itself) and remember the next time you make the same recipe using your particular cooking pot. You can also check manufacturer's instructions to slow cook this or overnight cook it (depending on when and how you will be serving this) or for general tips regarding the specific cookbook. All these cooking options are terrific, but they are not one-pot-fits-all recipes so remember to fiddle and adjust before you have perfection!

Famous Sweet and Sour Meatballs

There are meatball recipes and there are meatball recipes; this one breaks the mold. It uses two secret (pantry handy) ingredients that ensure these meatballs are zesty and full of bite. This is a dish that's equally at home on the Shabbat table, or at Rosh Hashanah and Passover. Whenever you make them, count on making two batches since people tend to sneak off with a taste here and there until there's none left for the meal!

* Citric acid or sour salt is available at King Arthur Flour, Amazon or in kosher food sections.

In a 4-quart saucepan, over low to medium heat, stir the cranberry sauce, tomato soup, ketchup, brown sugar, lemon juice, ginger ale, and wine and heat to just simmer.

Meanwhile, in a large bowl, combine the ground beef, egg, bread crumbs, onion and seasonings. Form into 1-inch balls.

Place the meatballs in the simmering sauce and let simmer on very low for one hour. Add in the citric acid, as per taste.

Serves 4-6

1 can jellied cranberry sauce

1 10 oz. can tomato soup

¾ cup ketchup

¼ cup brown sugar

2 teaspoons fresh lemon juice

½ cup ginger ale or cola

¼ cup red wine

1½ pound medium ground beef

1 egg

½ cup bread crumbs or matzoh meal

½ small onion, finely minced

¾ teaspoon salt

¼ teaspoon pepper

½ teaspoon citric acid or sour salt *

Sephardic Kitchen Spiced Meatballs

Here's yet another approach to meatballs and why not? The Jewish fondness, as with many cultures, for minced meat, generously spiced, go back to the days when a little meat had to go a long way. Creative ways with spices made meatballs a great vehicle and chef-proving ground. The Famous Sweet and Sour Meatballs in this chapter are clearly East European (leaning towards Russian and Polish roots), but this approach is clearly from the Sephardic kitchen.

Meatballs

1 pound hamburger meat

1 egg

3 tablespoons breadcrumbs or matzoh meal

2 cloves garlic, finely minced

Salt, pepper

1 28 ounce whole plum tomatoes

2 tablespoons pine nuts, finely chopped

2 tablespoons minced parsley

½ teaspoon mint

¼ teaspoon cayenne

1 teaspoon cumin

2 tablespoons extra virgin olive oil

Sauce Part

1 small onion, finely chopped

2 cloves garlic, finely minced

1 28 ounce whole plum tomatoes

3/8 teaspoon cinnamon

½ cup water or beef broth

1 tablespoon honey

1 tablespoon pomegranate molasses or balsamic vinegar

2 tablespoons finely minced parsley

For the Meatballs, in a medium bowl, combine the meat, egg, breadcrumbs, garlic, pine nuts, parsley, mint, cayenne, and cumin. Form mixture into one-inch balls. Heat the oil in a large, deep skillet over medium heat, and brown the meatballs about 15 minutes. Remove meatballs from skillet and set aside.

For the sauce, in the same skillet, add the onion, garlic, salt, pepper and brown lightly for five minutes. Add the tomatoes and stir and then add the cinnamon, water or beef broth, honey, molasses or vinegar and parsley. Add the meatballs to the sauce. Simmer over low heat, lightly covered, 30-45 minutes.

Serves 4-5

Friday Night Classic Beef Shabbat Cholent

The trick with cholent or the traditional, long-cooking Shabbat stew is not keeping the beef (or chicken parts) in large chunks to best withstand the long braising. The beef here stays moist and the lengthy cooking will ensure it's tender.

Place the beans into a 6-quart Dutch oven and cover with water. Allow to soak overnight and drain before proceeding with recipe. If you do not have time to pre-soak the beans, you can make the recipe anyway, but you will find you have to add more broth or liquid as it cooks, and it will take longer to cook for the beans will require more cooking time to soften.

Preheat oven to 325°. Place the beans in a 6-quart Dutch oven or casserole that that has a snug cover, add in the barley, potatoes, meat, onion, salt, pepper, paprika, onion powder, garlic powder, garlic, wine, ketchup and broth. Stir to blend. Cover and place in oven.

Slow bake until meat is tender, about 3-4 hours or more. Check the cholent every 30-45 minutes and add a small amount of water or stock as required, to ensure the cholent doesn't dry out and the beans and barley have enough liquid to cook in. You don't want the dish to dry out, but you also don't want to flood this into a liquid/gravy-based stew. It is a moist but solid dish. It might take you a few times to get this perfect.

Serves 6-8

½ cup dried kidney beans

½ cup dried lima beans

½ cup dried navy beans

½ cup pearl barley

6 medium potatoes peeled

1 pound stew meat or lean beef cubes

1 medium onion peeled, halved

1¼ teaspoon salt

¼ teaspoon pepper

2 tablespoons paprika

1 teaspoon onion powder

1 teaspoon garlic powder

3 cloves of garlic, finely minced

1/3 cup red wine

¼ cup ketchup

3-4 cups beef broth

BBQ Dry Rub Rib Style Brisket

This recipe is outstanding with ribs, but it also makes an exceptional 'rib' style tasting brisket for people who say they're not 'big' on brisket; this is a game changer! This will change your mind. The easy dry rub is key, the slow roasting, and final mop or glazing is what makes these special. It also is the perfect brisket for Brisket Sliders and if you do this on the outdoor BBQ, if it's a hot Rosh Hashanah (Indian Fall) you'll appreciate cooking this outdoors.

Brisket Dry Rub

1 4-5 pound brisket

1/3 cup brown sugar

5 teaspoons salt

5 teaspoons paprika

1 tablespoon chili powder

¾ teaspoon garlic powder

1½ teaspoons onion powder

¼ teaspoon cumin

1 teaspoon black pepper

¼ teaspoon cayenne pepper

Mop

1 12 oz. can root beer

1 12 oz. can cola drink

2 tablespoons steak sauce

½ cup BBQ sauce

¼ cup honey or molasses

½ cup brown sugar

½ cup ketchup

½ teaspoon liquid smoke *, optional

*Optional –for indoor roasting and only if you want the smoky taste

One to two days before, place brown sugar, salt, paprika, chili powder, garlic powder, onion powder, cumin, black pepper and cayenne in a small bowl and mix to blend. Pat all over brisket. Wrap in plastic wrap and refrigerate overnight (or up to 48 hours).

Preheat oven to 325°. Prepare the roasting pan by covering thoroughly with aluminum foil for easier clean up. Place brisket in a shallow baking dish and bake uncovered, 3- 4 hours until very tender.

Meanwhile, make the mop. Place all of the ingredients for the mop in a 4-quart pot or larger and cook over medium-high heat. Bring the contents of the pot to a boil, stirring often to dissolve the sugar. Once the mixture has come to a boil, reduce the heat to medium and allow the mixture to reduce to a thickened consistency by keeping it on low. Two hours before the brisket is fully cooked, start basting it every 20 minutes with the mop. Turn over the brisket and baste the bottom at least one time. When the brisket is about done (it will be fork tender), drizzle the last on the mop on top.

Serves 6-8

Shabbat Red Wine Brisket with Caramelized Onions and Mushrooms

Not only does this roast beef taste out of this world, it needs only one long, slow bake. No bake, chill, and re-slice. Who has time? I finally figured this out during a frantic week of High Holidays and limited oven space. A long, slow, gentle bake yields a tender, deeply flavorful roast and there's no need to slice and re-braise. It's a one-shot deal.

Preheat oven to 350°. Place meat on a large piece of foil and place in a large roasting pan.

In a large non-stick fry pan, over low heat, in the oil, slowly sauté the onions until they are softened and barely caramelized, about 15 minutes. Season with salt, pepper and then add the garlic. Cook to soften garlic, another five minutes. Stir in paprika, onion powder, and garlic powder. Spread this on top of the meat. Then, in order given, drizzle the red wine, beef bouillon, ketchup, tomato soup on top and around the meat. On top of the roast, dust on the dry mushroom or beef gravy powder, parsley, lemon juice and vinegar and last, scatter sliced mushrooms on top and around the meat.

Cover the brisket lightly in foil. Reduce heat to 325° and roast for 5-7 hours or until fork tender. (You can time this before the meal in time to serve, or make it a day ahead and reheat, sliced first or reheated as a whole roast). For the last 30 minutes, remove the foil and allow top of meat to crisp slightly.

If brisket needs more pan juices, add a few tablespoons of ketchup, and ¼ cup each of red wine or beef bouillon and water. To thicken pan juices, remove the meat and heat up the juices in the pan until they reduce and thicken.

Serves 10-14

4 medium onions sliced

2-4 tablespoons vegetable oil

Salt, pepper

4 cloves garlic, finely minced

2 tablespoons paprika

1 tablespoon onion powder

1 tablespoon garlic powder

1 4-5 pound beef brisket

1 cup sweet red wine

1 cup liquid beef broth

½ cup ketchup

1 can tomato soup

1 package dry mushroom sauce or beef gravy, optional

3 tablespoons fresh parsley, minced

1 tablespoon fresh lemon juice

1 tablespoon wine vinegar

2 cups sliced mushrooms

Korean Braised Siracha Brisket and Tri-Colour Asian Coleslaw

This is so festive, and I would serve it for Hanukkah, Purim or Shabbat. The trend of Korean BBQ with a homey brisket makes perfect sense. The side coleslaw is a cooling counterpoint. The New York Times is known for this recipe and it's adapted here (i.e. for one thing, there's no fish sauce) for the kosher table. Leftovers would be perfect for Brisket Sliders.

Brisket

1 4-5 pound brisket, cut into 3-4 pieces

1 tablespoon chili flakes

1 tablespoon paprika

2½ teaspoons salt

½ teaspoon black pepper

3 tablespoons vegetable oil

1 large onion, diced

4 garlic cloves, minced

1 tablespoons fresh minced ginger

1 cup beer

½ cup orange juice or apple juice

¼ cup Thai or Korean chili paste or Siracha sauce

2 tablespoons ketchup

2 tablespoons soy sauce

2 tablespoons brown sugar

1½ teaspoons sesame oil

Tri Colour Asian Coleslaw

3 cups shredded green cabbage

2 cups shredded purple cabbage

2 cups shredded carrots

¼ cup vegetable oil

1 tablespoon sesame seed oil

Juice of one lime

½ teaspoon salt

3 tablespoons brown sugar

2 teaspoons minced garlic

1 tablespoon minced fresh ginger

2 tablespoons black sesame seeds, optional

2 tablespoons minced cilantro

An hour before roasting, rub the sections of brisket with the chili flakes, paprika, salt and pepper. Refrigerate. Preheat oven to 325°.

Heat the oil in a large non-skillet or large cast iron pan and a piece at a time the meat, two minutes a side. Transfer to a large roasting pan. To the skillet, on medium heat, add the onion and cook to soften a few minutes. Stir in garlic and ginger and then the beer, orange juice, chili paste (or Siracha), ketchup, soy sauce, brown sugar and sesame oil. Spread this over the meat. Roast until tender, 3-4 hours.

For the coleslaw, mix all ingredients in a large bowl and refrigerate until serving time.

Once the meat is done, remove from pan and cook drippings on stove top to thicken to a sauce. Slice the meat and spoon the sauce over the slices. Serve with coleslaw and fresh challah rolls.

Serves 8-10

Guinness Braised Brisket

There are countless ways to make corned beef, from deli style to an Irish wash day classic. This one features a healthy dose of Guinness beer and is one of my favourites. You might wonder what a Guinness recipe is doing in a Jewish cookbook, but it's a salute to my late Uncle Jack Boness. He came to Canada from his native Ireland and was clearly as mindfully Jewish as any person as I ever met. Loved and respected by all for his good nature (and dapper bearing), Uncle Jack spoke Yiddish with an Irish brogue that was barely comprehensible (to me), but his warmth was undisputed.

1 4-5 pound corned beef (already corned with spices and salt)

¾ cup brown sugar, packed

1 12 ounce can of Guinness or other strong, dark beer

1 cup water or apple juice

Preheat oven to 325°.

If the corned beef is heavily spiced, brush or lightly rinse off the excess spices. If only a little spice is left on its surface, leave as is.

Place the corned beef in a roasting pan that just fits the roast – don't put it in too-large a pan or the liquid will evaporate too fast. Rub the brown sugar all over the meat. Then gently drizzle the beer all over it and add the water or apple juice. Cover lightly with foil and roast until tender, 4-5 hours.

Serve with braised cabbage, turnips and mashed potatoes or a potato kugel.

Serves 6-7

Famous Coca Cola Brisket

Things go better with a nice brisket almost any time of year. This cola-braised, uniquely spiced brisket is a slow-roast, favorite secret recipe. Southern Jewish cooks totally get cooking with cola.

Preheat oven to 350°. Place meat in a large roasting pan and sprinkle onions on top and around sides. Season well with salt, pepper and the paprika.

In a medium bowl or 4-cup measuring cup, mix ketchup with tomato sauce, barbecue sauce, steak sauce, hot water and cola. Pour over the meat. Top the meat with the minced garlic. Cover pan lightly with foil. Roast 3-3½ hours, basting every 20 to 30 minutes. Once the meat is ready, slice it and put back in the gravy. Before serving, reheat at 325° for an hour to further braise and tenderize the meat.

Serves 6 to 8

1 4-5 pound beef brisket

1 cup chopped onions

Salt, pepper

2 tablespoons paprika

4 garlic cloves, finely minced

½ cup ketchup

½ cup tomato sauce

¼ cup BBQ sauce

1 tablespoon steak sauce

¼ cup hot water

2 cups cola beverage

4 cloves minced garlic

Forty Cloves of Garlic Brisket

This is a '70s iconic recipe that originally called for stewing meat. I prefer it with brisket which takes well to a slow roast with a ton of garlic which mellows out as it bakes. If you have fresh thyme and rosemary on hand, that's best and you can use a little more than the amounts stipulated for dry herbs.

1 4-5 pound beef brisket

2 tablespoons olive oil

Salt, pepper

40 large cloves garlic, peeled

1 large onion, coarsely chopped

¼ cup red wine vinegar

2 ½ cups beef stock

2 teaspoons oregano

1 teaspoon basil

¼ teaspoon thyme

¼ teaspoon dry rosemary

Preheat oven to 350°.

In a large roasting pan, place the brisket and smear with the olive oil and generously season with the salt and pepper. Sprinkle garlic and onions all over the meat. Drizzle on the red wine vinegar, beef stock, oregano, basil, thyme and rosemary. Cover lightly with foil.

Bake one hour at 350° and then lower temperature to 325° and bake another 1½-2 hours until the meat is fork tender. (While it cooks, add more water to ensure the roasting pan doesn't dry out).

Remove half the garlic cloves and onions and discard. To the pan, mash up garlic into the pan juices. Slice the brisket and place back in the pan, spooning sauce over slices. Serve (or reheat) with pan sauce.

Serves 8-10

Apple Cider Vinegar Brisket

Apple cider vinegar does wonders for everything and in this recipe, along with the balance of apple cider and some other good things, it adds a tangy taste to this tender brisket.

Preheat oven to 325°.

Slice the onions and apples and place them on the bottom of a large roasting pan. Place brisket on top of this; generously dust with salt and pepper. Then press on the onion powder, garlic powder, paprika, thyme and rosemary. Pour apple juice, cider vinegar, beef stock around sides of the meat and drizzle on BBQ sauce, molasses and honey to the liquid in the pan.

Cover and roast until tender 4-5 hours. If brisket seems to be cooking but pan juices evaporate, add a bit of apple juice and water or some beef stock.

Once brisket is cooked and cooled, slice thin and put the slices back in pan juice. Add more beef stock and wine (half each) as required to ensure there's sufficient pan liquid with which to braise the meat and preventing it from drying out sauce to allow the meat to braise. Return to oven and roast (at 325°) until tender, 1½- 2 hours.

Serves 8-10

1 medium onion, finely sliced

1 large apple, cored, peeled and sliced

1 4-5 pound beef brisket

2 teaspoons salt

½ teaspoon pepper

1 tablespoon onion powder

2 tablespoons garlic powder

3 tablespoons paprika

1/8 teaspoon thyme

1/8 teaspoon rosemary

1 cup apple juice or cider

¼ cup apple cider vinegar

¼ cup beef stock

2 tablespoons BBQ sauce

1 tablespoon molasses

2 tablespoons honey

Hickory Smoked Brisket

This brisket is appealingly sticky on the outside, pinkish on the inside, and suffused with deep barbecue and smoke flavor. It's delicious hot with additional barbecue sauce or thinly sliced and piled high on grilled garlic French rolls. Cold, this is a treat on soft Italian buns or crusty mini-baguettes, alongside a trough of coleslaw and an old-fashioned jug of real lemonade.

6 large garlic cloves minced

1 small onion, minced

1 tablespoon salt

1 tablespoon paprika

1 tablespoon garlic powder

½ teaspoon pepper

½ cup barbecue sauce

2 tablespoons steak sauce

2 teaspoons Dijon mustard

¼ cup molasses

2 tablespoons honey

1 4-5 pound beef brisket

Preheat oven to 325°.

In a food processor, combine garlic, onions, and salt together to make a paste or blend as best you can. Stir in remaining ingredients. Place meat in a large roasting dish and smear marinade all over meat. Dust with a little more salt, pepper and paprika, if desired; the spices should be very thickly applied. Roast until tender, 3-4 hours. When meat is cool enough to be handled, slice about ¼ inch thick and lay out in a roasting pan. Top with about two cups of warm barbecue or pan juices (to make two cups). Warm in a slow oven, 325°, covered for about 2 hours to tenderize and thoroughly rewarm meat.

Makes 6-8 servings

Garlic Dijon Brisket

I love treating homey brisket with a French touch of Dijon and garlic. This brisket roasts to zesty perfection and really is as good hot as cold i.e. in sandwiches). This is based on a vintage recipe from my late mother-in-law Shirley Posluns, who made this with a different cut (a cross rib roast) and was legendary for her ability to make anything exceptionally flavorful. Her instincts in the kitchen were legend and this is one of her most iconic recipes.

Preheat oven to 375°. Place brisket in a shallow roasting pan. In a small bowl, make a paste by mixing the mustard with the garlic, garlic powder, some salt, black pepper, dry mustard, oil and paprika. Spread the garlic granules over top and sides.

Make additional paste if meat is not well covered. since the meat really must be thickly slathered and you can't really over-do it. To the pan, on side of roast, pour in water, wine, beef gravy mix and onion soup powder. Sprinkle top of roast generously with extra garlic and paprika. Cover roast with foil.

Roast at 375° for the first hour. Reduce temperature to 350° and continue roasting for a couple of hours (depending on desired doneness) - basting every so often, about 3-4 hours. Remove foil during last half hour of cooking.

Remove meat slice thinly. In the roasting pan, stir in mushroom soup with pan juices, mixing well. This thickened pan juice can be a side gravy.

Serves 8-10

1 4-5 pound beef brisket

1/3 cup Dijon mustard

10 large garlic cloves, minced

½ teaspoon black pepper

1 tablespoon garlic powder

1 tablespoon salt

½ teaspoon pepper

1 tablespoon dry mustard

2 tablespoons olive oil

1 tablespoon paprika

2 tablespoons dry garlic granules

1¼ cup water

½ cup red wine

1 packet beef gravy mix

1 packet dry onion soup

1 10 ounce can mushroom soup

Braised Short Ribs or Pot Roast

Back in the day, a lot of short rib recipes included convenience products such as onion soup powder, wine, and ketchup. Fifties and sixties housewives loved those timesaver and 'modern' ingredients. This healthier, retooled recipe for short ribs is still as old-fashioned as ever. Easy, deeply flavored, and extra tender, this is a '50s vintage pot roast vibe but with contemporary deliciousness. This recipe uses beer, but red wine can be swapped.

5 pounds beef short ribs

1 tablespoon salt

½ teaspoon pepper

1 tablespoon paprika

1 teaspoon dry mustard

2 teaspoons onion powder

1 tablespoon garlic powder

½ teaspoon thyme

2 medium onions, sliced

2 medium carrots, sliced

½ cup beef broth

1½ cup beer or beef broth

1 cup tomato sauce

1/3 cup BBQ sauce

6-8 large potatoes, quartered

Preheat oven to 350°. Place the pot roast or short ribs in a 6-8 quart heavy Dutch oven.

Coat with salt, pepper, paprika, dry mustard, onion powder, garlic powder, salt and pepper. Sprinkle on onions, carrots, and then add beef broth, beer, tomato sauce, and barbecue sauce.

Cover Dutch oven and roast 3-4 hours or until meat is tender. If sauce is evaporating too quickly as meat is braising, add ½ cup of beer or beef broth. During the last hour of cooking, scatter the potatoes around the meat.

Serves 4-6

American Deli Style Pastrami

A commercial corned eye of round or brisket makes this recipe a snap. You may also opt for the home corning method. A lot of time pastrami is made with the eye-of-round cut versus the brisket cut; both are great. I've included a smoker as well as a regular oven method in this recipe. If you have a corned beef, ignore the wet brine method as it's not necessary.

About 4-6 hours before smoking meat, remove from brine and pat dry. Sprinkle liberally with paprika. On each side of brisket, pat about 1/3-1/2 cup of prepared steak spices, pressing into meat. Wrap in a plastic bag or lots of wax paper and then wrap again, tightly in foil wrap. Refrigerate until ready to smoke.

If you are using a store bought, pre-corned brisket, rinse lightly and pat dry. Proceed as above, covering with paprika and spices. Commercially corned meat has saltpeter in it, so you can count on this brisket taking on a pinkish color.

For oven roasting, preheat oven to 350°. Place roast in roasting pan and cover lightly with foil. Roast 3-4 hours, basting every so often with pan juices; remove foil during last half hour of cooking.

For outdoor smoking, place meat on grill, cover smoker, and leave vents partially open. Make a double layer of briquettes and use about 3-4 large, pre-soaked, maple chunks Replace about 8-10 briquettes every 1½ hours and add additional wood chunks (about 4) as required - i.e. if you notice they are burning to ash and need replacing. Cook until meat thermometer registers about 145° (temperature will climb quickly at that point and final inside temperature will result in meat that is "Medium" cooked). Refrigerate meat overnight. Slice thinly and serve with deli style mustard on rye bread.

Serves 8-10

Wet Brine

1 4-5 pound eye-of-round cut beef roast or corned beef brisket

12 quarts water

1½ cups pickling salt

¼ cup pickling spices

¾ teaspoons salt peter, optional

Dry Spice

Paprika, for sprinkling

1/3 cup steak spices (such as McCormick's Grill Mates or Montreal Steak Spice)

Smoker preparation

Hickory or oak chunks, pre-soaked about an hour before

If you don't have a corned brisket, use the Wet Brine. For Wet Brine, mix brine ingredients together in a large casserole and place brisket in brine. Allow to brine two days in the fridge, turning over occasionally, to swish meat thoroughly through brine.

Montreal Smoked Meat Style Brisket

Penzey's Corned Beef Spices or McCormick's Montreal Smoked Meat Spices are pretty well all you need here (along with the beef). Essentially Montreal Smoked Meat has a dry rub marinade for a few days and then is smoked (and sometimes steamed for an hour before serving to plump it up). Here you have a choice of smoking it or oven roasting it.

Dry Spice

1 5-6 pound brisket

Paprika

½ cup, approximately, steak spices *

Liquid smoke

Smoker Preparation

Hickory or oak chunks pre-soaked in water one hour

* Such as McCormick's Montreal Steak Spice or Penzey's Bicentennial Rub

Three to four days before serving, coat the brisket with paprika and spices. Cover in foil and refrigerate 3-4 days.

For the smoker method, place meat on grill, cover smoker, and leave vents partially open. Make a double layer of briquettes and use about 3-4 large, pre-soaked, maple chunks Replace about 8-10 briquettes every 1½ hours and add additional wood chunks (about 4) as required - i.e. if you notice they are burning to ash and need replacing. Cook, until meat thermometer registers about 165° (temperature will climb quicker at that point and final inside temperature will result in meat that is "Medium" cooked) Refrigerate meat overnight. Slice thinly and serve with deli style mustard on rye bread.

For oven cooking, place the meat on a wire rack set over a foil-lined baking sheet. Drop a few drops of liquid smoke on meat. Cover with a tent of foil. Roast until meat tests done, about 3 hours.

Serves 8-10

Chapter Nine
Fish

Fish

Fish in the Jewish kitchen is a simple affair. Kosher laws negated the whole seafood category and so fresh water fish for the most part, are where most fish recipes for this chapter originate. Of course, Gefilte Fish is the crown to the fish throne but there are so many other delectable, healthy fish recipes to consider that are beautiful offerings, whatever the occasion.

Sweet Style Gefilte Fish

Be brave. You *can* make great, fresh, traditional gefilte fish. The big secret, despite the hype and myth is, if you can make hamburgers, you can make gefilte fish. This recipe is sweeter than some, and in my opinion, more flavourful than most. Your fish monger will prepare the ground fish; then all you do is season the minced fish as per recipe, form it into balls, simmer or poach in the fish broth. Then chill the fish, serve, and bask in the compliments. You may be the head honcho at Microsoft, but making gefilte fish will earn you *real* respect. Some guests may find this recipe uniquely sweet and peppery (but will eventually agree, give it a Passover or two, that this is about the best gefilte fish in the world). Inevitably, they will comment that it is not the style they are used to. They might even talk about it for months afterwards, but next year, they will not only beg to come to your Seder but implore you to share the recipe! My mother-in-law, Shirley Posluns taught me the recipe and she still makes it best. To get rid of the fish odour after this is done, just put some cut-up lemons in water in a bowl and simmer (or put a dish of lemons and water in the microwave for a few minutes) to bring a lemony freshness into a kitchen that otherwise will smell just a bit like a wharf (but it passes). Oh, and check out how to season raw gefilte fish in the recipe instructions. Whatever you do, don't taste the raw fish as my grandmother Annie Marks Goldman did. Family lore has it that Grandma Goldman got tapeworm from taste testing raw gefilte fish. I don't even know if that is true, but it has made great family history and a strong caution for proper raw fish seasoning methodology.

Sweet Style Gefilte Fish

If you can make hamburgers, you can make gefilte fish. To test the seasoning here's a great trick: remove two tablespoons of the raw fish mixture, wrap it in Saran wrap and microwave a few minutes. Cool, taste and then, using your palate and judgment, add whatever salt, pepper, or a bit of sugar to the raw fish batch as required. This is so good, that even commercial jarred horseradish wouldn't dim its impact.

Fish Broth

Extra fish bones (about a pound, tail, head, fish bones)

Water (4 quarts approximately)

2 or 3 small carrots, trimmed, in chunks

2 small ribs celery

2 or 3 small onions, quartered

2½ teaspoons salt

¼ teaspoon pepper

4 teaspoons whole black peppercorns

½ cup sugar

¼ cup parsley coarsely diced

Fish

1 pound dory, ground

½ pound whitefish, ground

½ pound pike, ground

3 eggs

1 medium onion, finely minced

1 large carrot, finely minced

1 very small stalk celery, finely minced

1/3 cup matzoh meal

¾ cup ice water

2¼ teaspoons salt

½ teaspoon pepper

1/3 cup sugar

For the fish broth, place the water and fish parts in a 7-8 quart wide pot. Add the carrots, celery, onion, salt, pepper, peppercorns sugar and parsley. Bring to a boil and reduce to simmer. Let simmer 30-45 minutes, straining away any foam that might form, while assembling fish balls.

For the gefilte fish itself, place the fish in a food processor (even though it is ground) and blend briefly to fluff up. You can also do this in a large wood bowl and with a hand mincer and chop or mince briskly to lighten the fish, slowly adding about ¼ cup of ice water as you do this.

Make sure the fish is minced well, then mix in remaining ingredients (as if you were making burgers), adding a bit more ice water in small amounts to fluff up the fish if it looks too pasty. If mixture is very loose (it is a loose mixture, but it will hold it shape, more it less if you handle it tenderly), add more matzoh meal. Chilling will help. Shape into balls or nice ovals. To form, use wet hands (re-dipping in a bowl of cold water as necessary).

Before adding fish balls, remove larger pieces of fish bones, tail, etc. (leave vegetables in the broth).

Bring broth to a boil again and very gently add the fish balls and simmer on lowest heat possible, semi-covered for 1-2 hours. With a slotted spoon, remove the gefilte pieces from the broth to a dish you can refrigerate, covered. Spoon a little bit of broth over the fish. Chill well, at least overnight, before serving. Serve with horseradish.

Makes 16-20 pieces

Sweet and Hot Horseradish

Make this just once and you will never buy it from the store again, nor have to depend on the one relative that still makes it (unless you want to because it's a wonderful family tradition). Nothing beats horseradish autonomy and know-how. A really good potato peeler (Good Grips is a fine one) helps make short work of removing the tough exterior skin of the horseradish root. Wear goggles to make this and keep the windows open as you work. I also suggest latex gloves (pharmacies sell them by the boxful) for handling this pungent condiment (the gloves are also perfect for gefilte fish-making or matzoh balls). My Uncle Bern taught me, a few hints at a time, over many Passovers, how to make horseradish. Our family had many nieces, but only one horseradish maker among them: the baker girl.

With a food processor, using a fine shredding wheel or disc, shred the horseradish quite fine. (You can also hand shred this, but this method of shredding, then pulverizing in a food processor works very well). Next, shred the beets directly on top. Remove from processor and install the regular blade.

Process the horseradish and beets, adding vinegar, salt and sugar mid-way, to make a pasty sauce. Taste test a bit of the mixture on matzoh (or a piece of gefilte fish if you have some nearby). Adjust seasonings and process to combine. Let mixture stand 30 minutes and then cover, and store refrigerated up to 10-14 days before serving. Flavor will mellow as horseradish matures.

Makes about 2 cups

1 large horseradish root, trimmed and peeled

2 medium beets, peeled

½ to 1 cup white vinegar

4-5 teaspoons salt

½ to ¾ cup sugar

Tuna Patties

Sometimes something simple is all you want. These tuna patties harken back to grandma's quick lunch for the 'kids' or a deli standby. I don't know why they went out of style. Paired with a whole-wheat pita and some minced pickles, slivered lettuce and red cabbage and a touch of dill, mayo or tartar sauce, these are outstanding. The Old Bay Seasoning is a treasure of an ingredient and is usually found in the spice aisle.

2 5-6 ounce cans (5-6 oz.) white tuna, preferably flaked, water packed

2 teaspoons Dijon mustard

1 tablespoon mayonnaise

1 egg, optional

½ cup minced white bread or challah, or bread crumbs

1 teaspoon lemon zest

1 tablespoon fresh lemon juice

2 tablespoon fresh minced parsley

1 tablespoon each fresh minced dill chives

2 tablespoon minced onion or green onion

¼ cup minced celery

¼ teaspoon (or more) Old Bay seasoning, optional

¼ teaspoon celery powder

1 teaspoon hot sauce

Place all ingredients in a large bowl and mix together until mixture can be formed into patties.

If tuna is not flaked, gently flake in a food processor first.

For into four patties and chill an hour (this is optional, but it's helpful).

Heat olive oil in a non-stick skillet or a cast iron fry pan on medium high. Gently place patties in pan and cook until browned, about 3-4 minutes per side.

Serves 4

Tuna and Brie Sandwiches

This takes diner food up a notch to sophistication but happily, it's still fast and easy. You can also make these sandwiches in an open-faced rendition and just broil briefly to melt the cheese before serving.

Smear or brush each piece of bread on both sides with some olive oil or butter. Rub the garlic over each side of the slices. Set aside.

In a food processor, put all ingredients in at once and pulse to make a coarse but combined filling. Adjust seasonings. (Add a bit more mayonnaise if mixture is dry.)

Pat equal amounts of the tuna filling on a bread slice. Top each with the 3-4 slices of brie and top with remaining slices of bread.

Preheat a non-stick skillet. Add the butter or olive oil and let heat 20-30 seconds. Place the sandwiches down firmly in the pan. Using 3-4 dinner plates as weights, press down the sandwiches. Cook over medium low heat and then, turn over to brown other side of each sandwich.

Serves 2

Sandwich Prep

4 large slices sourdough or country bread

Olive oil or unsalted butter

1 large garlic clove, minced

6-8 ¼ inch slices Brie cheese

Tuna Filling

3 7-ounce cans or equivalent, white flaked tuna packed in water

1/3 cup mayonnaise

1 tablespoon Dijon mustard

1 tablespoon fresh lemon juice

Salt, pepper, hot sauce

¼ cup very minced celery

1 tablespoon very finely minced onion

1 tablespoon each minced fresh parsley and dill

1 tablespoon capers, optional

2 tablespoons optional, pitted, sliced black olives

Jewish Greek Fish

Sunny, simple and flavorful – what else would you expect from a quick Greek fish recipe? Have your fish monger gut and trim the fish if you prefer filets over whole fish. This is perfect whether you choose bass, snapper, sole or even wild salmon. This recipe is a salute to a little restaurant in Montreal that seems to have a dual Jewish Greek heritage going on (as well as a tell-tale cookbook called The Jewish Greek Cookbook on a shelf near the cash)

1 large whole fish (2–3 pounds), such as bass, snapper or trout, butterflied, boned and gutted

2 cup cherry tomatoes, halved

¼ cup extra virgin olive oil

1 tablespoon white vinegar

2 tablespoons fresh lemon juice

2 teaspoons minced fresh hot chili, such as jalapeno

1 tablespoons fresh oregano, finely minced

4 cloves garlic, thinly sliced

Salt, pepper

1 large lemon, thinly sliced

3 tablespoons minced parsley

Sprinkle inside of fish with some salt and pepper. Set aside.

In a medium bowl, toss the tomatoes, 2 tablespoons of the oil, vinegar, lemon juice, chili, oregano, most of the garlic, and a dusting of salt and pepper. Let stand 15 minutes.

Heat a large non-stick pan or cast-iron pan with the remaining olive oil. Add the fish and sauté 15-20 minutes. Gently turn, toss on tomato mixture and remaining garlic, and cook the other side 8 minutes. Before serving, adjust seasons (adding more salt or herbs) and garnish with rosemary or parsley. Serve with rice or lemon roasted potatoes.

Serves 2-3

Pickled Salmon

Everyone should have such a dish on stand-by. It's great luncheon fare with its pungent sweet, tangy and peppery flavor. This is a recipe that goes back 3-4 generations of great Jewish cooks.

In a 3 or 4-quart saucepan, place vinegar, water, sugar, ketchup or chili sauce, salt. Bring to a boil. Add vinegar and spices and reduce heat to simmer. Add slices of fish. Simmer about 8-10 minutes.

Chill overnight before serving.

Serves 4-6

1 cup vinegar

1 cup water

½ cup sugar

1¼ cup ketchup or chili sauce

1 teaspoon salt

6 sliced onions

2 tablespoons pickling spices

1½ pounds salmon

Poached Bar Mitzvah or Wedding Salmon and Two Sauces

I love the elegance of poached salmon along with how easy it is to make. If you don't have a poacher, just circle the fish 'in' on itself in a wide pot. This is fail-proof and just the thing for almost any Jewish holiday, but also for home weddings or bar or bat mitzvah buffet tables.

1 5-6 pounds whole salmon

2 cups white wine

1 medium onion sliced

3 carrots, cut in chunks

3 ribs celery, cut in chunks

2-3 tablespoons kosher salt

1 teaspoon pepper

¼ cup minced fresh parsley

2 tablespoons fresh dill, minced

Water

Place salmon in poaching pot or large (more wide than deep) and just cover with water. Turn the fish around so that it is end to end (as if it were chasing its own tail). Add wine and remaining ingredients. Bring to a boil, reduce heat and simmer until done - about 30-40 minutes (about 10 minutes per pound. Turn off burner and let fish cool 20 minutes. Carefully remove from poacher and place on platter. Cover and refrigerate. Next day, gently remove skin. Present on a bed of dark greens. Garnish with parsley sprigs and lemon slices.

Serves 8-12

Two Sauces for Cold Salmon

I like choices and these two quick side sauces for poached, chilled salmon are both easy and elegent. I always offer both.

For either sauce, combine ingredients in a small bowl and blend until smooth. Chill and serve on side with salmon.

Red Sauce

1 cup mayonnaise

½ cup ketchup or chilli sauce

Dijon Sauce

1 cup mayonnaise

1/3 cup Dijon mustard

1 tablespoon minced dill

White Fish Salad

Among other salads and spreads, Jewish Hall of Famers munched on a delicate fish salad, made with smoky whitefish and herbs. You can use lite sour cream and lite mayonnaise. Serve with black bread or crackers, or mini pitas. This is also a great brunch dish or appetizer.

2 generous cups smoked white-fish, coarsely chopped or flaked

½ cup mayonnaise

Juice of half a lemon

Salt, pepper,

2 tablespoons minced chives

2 tablespoons parsley, finely minced

1/3 cup sour cream

Trim the fish of bones and skin and be careful to remove all small bones. Gently flake fish into small chunks. Place in a bowl and toss with remaining ingredients.

Chill well.

Serves 4-6

Maple Teriyaki Salmon

Broiled or grilled, this makes an outstanding, light entree of fish. The maple brings out the subtle salmon taste and helps it caramelize on the edges just so. Serve with asparagus and wild rice. Maple, soya and sesame collide in a West meets East with Northern Exposure accent. Increasingly, you can find kosher maple syrup (usually from Vermont).

In a medium bowl, mix all ingredients. Place salmon in a shallow dish and cover well with marinade (turning once). Marinate 1 to 3 hours. Grill or broil until done, basting with marinade (but once fish is halfway done, stop basting).

Serves 4

Fish

4 8-10 ounce salmon steaks

Marinade

1/3 cup pure maple syrup

2 tablespoons brown sugar

1/3 cup white wine

1 teaspoon sesame seed oil

3 tablespoons soya sauce

2 scallions, minced

1 teaspoon fresh ginger root, minced

2 garlic cloves, minced

Salt, pepper

Salmon in a Package with Green Herb Slather Marinade

———————— ❖ ————————

I love this herb coating on fresh salmon steaks or filets. Make this in the oven or in papiotte, a parchment paper envelope. This is one of my favorite lunch choices. The marinade lasts for a week or so for using on tossed, boiled new potatoes or in vinaigrette or more fish fare. Serve this dish with wild rice or lemony couscous.

Salmon filets or steaks, as required (8-10 ounce filet per serving)

1 medium yellow onion, coarsely chopped

1 cup fresh basil leaves

½ cup fresh Italian parsley

1 tablespoon fresh rosemary leaves

1 tablespoon fresh sage leaves

3 tablespoons fresh dill

½ teaspoon fresh mint

1 tablespoons fresh lemon zest

1 tablespoons fresh lemon juice

4 garlic cloves, peeled

1 cup light olive oil

½ teaspoon salt

¼ teaspoon pepper

Place the onion, all the herbs, lemon zest, lemon juice, and garlic in a food processor. Pulse several times to chop. Add oil, salt and pepper. Puree and refrigerate or use right away. To make the fish, coat a salmon filet thirty minutes to 2 hours ahead in the about ½ cup of marinade.

Preheat oven to 400°.

Line a large baking sheet or rectangular roasting dish with foil and then parchment paper to line the bottom. Wrap each filet in parchment paper, making a sealed envelope (seam side down on the baking sheet). Place fish in oven, as close to heat sources as possible and bake until done, without the parchment, about 12 minutes or until fillets are done (they will flake apart).

Serves 3-4

Chapter Ten
Vegetarian Dishes

Vegetarian Recipes

Not everyone likes meat and even those that do appreciate a non-meat option on occasions. For those people (I count myself among the occasional vegetarian/vegan crowd), I am delighted to share some of my vegetarian options with a Jewish cuisine spin. Cabbage Rolls, Quinoa Cutlets and Vegetarian Sweet and Sour Meatballs are just some offerings. These are all main dishes, or you can offer one of them to your guests as a side dish alongside whatever else (beef or chicken) is being served.

Sweet and Sour Quinoa Meatballs

I use a mixture of red and white quinoa for this. Citric acid looks a bit like salt but provides a nice zap of tartness to any dish. It's a bubbie-era secret ingredient. You can find it on Amazon. Check out the Passover version of these in the Passover Chapter.

In a large bowl, mix all ingredients for the meatballs together. Chill twenty minutes.

Preheat oven to 350°. Line a large baking sheet with parchment paper and smear with 2-3 tablespoons olive oil.

For the Sweet and Sour Sauce, in a medium saucepan, mix together the cranberry sauce, grape jam ketchup, brown sugar, lemon juice, ginger-ale, water and citric acid; heat over low heat while preparing quinoa balls.

Shape the quinoa mixture into 1-inch balls. Place on baking sheet and bake until browned, 20-25 minutes. Remove and place in Sweet and Sour Sauce and cook on low heat for 30-60 minutes.

Serves 5-6

Quinoa Meatballs

2-3 tablespoons oil

2 cups cooked quinoa

¼ cup shredded carrot

2 tablespoons onion, finely minced

2 tablespoons parsley, finely minced

½ cup grated white cheddar cheese, optional

2 tablespoons Parmesan cheese, optional

1 teaspoon minced garlic

½ teaspoon onion powder

¼ teaspoon pepper

¾ teaspoon salt

¾ cup breadcrumbs

3 eggs

Sweet and Sour Sauce

½ can jellied cranberry sauce

½ cup grape jam

¾ cup ketchup

¼ cup brown sugar

2 teaspoons fresh lemon juice

½ cup ginger ale

¼ cup water

3/8 teaspoon citric acid, optional

Stuffed Eggplants with Herbed Bulgur

This is a meal by itself, but also a great side dish with a Mediterranean vibe. I like this for Shabbat or Sukkot or even Thanksgiving.

6 small eggplants

5 tablespoons olive oil

1 teaspoon salt

½ teaspoon black pepper

1 teaspoon za'atar spice

1 cup dry bulgur wheat

½ cup fresh parsley leaves

¼ cup fresh cilantro leaves

¼ cup scallions, thinly sliced

¼ cup toasted pine nuts

¼ cup pomegranate seeds

½ lemon, zested, juiced

Finishing Touches

Minced mint, cilantro, parsley, pomegranate seeds

Preheat oven to 350°.

Wash the eggplants and slice them in half lengthwise. Using a paring knife, score the eggplant halves with diagonal cross-hatches just on the surface. Drizzle each eggplant half with about a half-tablespoon of olive oil each. Season with the salt, pepper and za'atar spice. Bake, cut-side up, for about 45 minutes or until the eggplants are completely soft.

While the eggplants are baking, place the dry bulgur in a medium-sized bowl and pour boiling water over to cover by ½ inch. Place a kitchen towel over the bowl and let stand for 10 minutes. After 10 minutes, remove the towel and fluff the bulgur with a fork. (If the grain isn't tender enough, let it stand, covered, a few more minutes; it should absorb all the water)

Finely chop the parsley and cilantro. In a large bowl, mix the bulgur with the parsley, cilantro, scallions, pine nuts, pomegranate seeds, lemon zest and juice, and remaining 2 table-spoons of olive oil. Place the cooked eggplants on to a platter and spoon the bulgur salad over the eggplants. Garnish with mint, cilantro, parsley and pomegranate seeds.

Serves 6-9

Nut Roast

This is vegetarian (vegan if you omit the cheese and eggs, which you can) and as meaty-tasting as a regular meat loaf making it soulfully delicious for all sorts of dinner guests. Serve it as a meatloaf with sides of quinoa and steamed asparagus. It's great for Shabbat or as high holiday main dish. Despite its hippie rep as a vegetarian classic, this is surprisingly 'bubbie' tasting, but then what comfort food isn't?

Preheat oven to 350°. Line a baking sheet with parchment paper and spray a 9 by 5 inch loaf pan with non-stick cooking spray. Place nuts on baking sheet and bake 10-12 minutes. Remove nuts from pan and set aside; place loaf pan on baking sheet.

In a large, non-stick frying pan, over medium heat, add the oil, add the onion, celery, carrot and red pepper and sauté until softened, about 5 minutes. Add in the mushrooms and sauté until softened, about 8-10 minutes on low, adding in water a bit at a time, to help things cook without sticking.

Remove from heat and stir in tomato paste, parsley, oregano, rosemary, thyme, sage, Worcestershire sauce, Maggi seasoning, and gravy browning and stir well. Add in eggs, lentils, nuts, breadcrumbs, and cheddar cheese. Pour or spoon into loaf pan. Lightly brush with barbecue sauce or ketchup.

Bake until set and firm, about 45-50 minutes. Cool 20 minutes before serving or refrigerate and heat in slices. Serve with whatever condiments you prefer (cranberry sauce, ketchup or Dijon mustard, etc.).

Serves 6-8

1¼ cups walnuts, finely chopped
¼ cup light olive oil
1 large onion, finely chopped
2 sticks celery, finely chopped
1 large carrot, shredded
1 red pepper, finely chopped
2 cloves garlic, finely minced
2½ cups mushrooms, finely chopped
2 tablespoons tomato paste
¼ cup parsley, finely minced
½ teaspoon oregano
¼ teaspoon rosemary
¼ teaspoon thyme
1/8 teaspoon sage
1 teaspoon Worcestershire sauce
2 teaspoons Maggie Seasoning, optional
1 teaspoon gravy browning such as Kitchen Bouquet, optional
3 eggs
½ cup vegetable broth
½ cup mashed red lentils
1 cup breadcrumbs
1 cup shredded cheddar cheese

Best Ever Tomato Tart

If you've never had a fresh tomato tart, you've been missing out. This is a taste experience that amalgamates pizza, quiche and a savory tart – it is utterly fantastic. If you want to speed this up, swap in the butter pastry dough for bought puff pastry. This is recommended for anytime, but especially welcome at Shavuot, Shabbat luncheon, Sukkot or as a vegetarian main dish.

Butter Pastry

2 cups all-purpose flour

¾ cup unsalted butter

1 teaspoon sugar

1 teaspoon salt

1 tablespoon lemon juice

½ cup ice water

Tomato Basil Tomato Topping

½ cup chopped fresh basil

1 cup chopped fresh parsley

3 large garlic cloves, peeled

1 tablespoon fresh thyme leaves

Salt, pepper

½ cup olive oil

2½ pounds medium size tomatoes, sliced

½ pound medium cheddar cheese, grated

¼ pound fontina cheese, grated

4 tablespoons Dijon mustard

½ cup Parmesan cheese, grated

For the pastry, place the flour in a large mixer bowl. With a pastry blender, or your hands, cut in the butter until mixture is crumbly – a somewhat lumpy, bumpy mixture of little and larger lumps of flour-covered-butter. Make a well in center of flour mixture and stir in the sugar, and salt, and lemon juice. Drizzle in most of ice water and using a fork or fingers, toss mixture together to moisten flour. Stir to make a soft mass and pat into a rough dough. Add remaining (or additional) ice water as required to make sure dough sticks together. Turn out onto a lightly floured work surface. Knead very briefly into a smooth, cohesive dough. Place dough in a Ziploc bag and refrigerate the dough at least one hour or up to two days.

For the Tomato Topping, in a food processor, add the basil, parsley, thyme, garlic and season with salt and pepper. Add olive oil and blend to mince up garlic and mix ingredients, about 1-2 minutes. Prepare tomatoes and place in a large bowl and cover with herb marinade and toss to blend.

Roll out dough on a lightly floured work surface to an 11 by 17 inch rectangle. Transfer it to a parchment paper lined baking sheet. Preheat oven to 400°. Place a piece of parchment lightly on the dough and then another baking sheet. Bake 10-15 minutes to just dry out the crust. Cool slightly and then brush the dough with the Dijon mustard. On top of the dough, arrange half the cheddar and fontina. Arrange the herbed-tomato slices in rows on top of the pastry add the rest of the grated cheddar and fontina and last, sprinkle on with the Parmesan. Bake, immediately lowering temperature to 350°, 30-35 minutes until the edges of the pastry are browned and top is bubbling (tomatoes are softened, and cheese is melted and golden).

Cool slightly and cut into large squares to serve (good warm or room temperature or re-heated)

Makes 6-8 servings

Bistro Style Zucchini Lasagna Primavera

You can use regular boxed lasagne noodles or fresh ones. If you can find a more ambrosial-tasting lasagne recipe, please share it! Sometimes I make this with half zucchini and spinach as a garden-fresh variation.

Garlic Béchamel

10 – 12 ounces green spinach lasagna noodles (about 9 strips – 2½ inches by 8 inches or so)

2 tablespoons light olive oil

3 tablespoons flour

½ cup vegetable broth

1 tablespoon white wine

2 cloves garlic, finely minced

3/8 teaspoon salt

¼ teaspoon white pepper

1 cup milk

4 tablespoons chevre

Sauce

2½ cups marinara sauce

Filling

4 cups shredded zucchini (or steamed)

1 cup minced cooked broccoli

2 cups baby spinach

1 cup fresh basil leaves, minced or cut by hand into small pieces

¼ cup parsley, finely minced

1 tablespoon sun dried tomato pesto

1 tablespoon basil pesto

½ teaspoon dry Italian spices

1 cup low-fat ricotta

3 cups mozzarella cheese, finely shredded

2 tablespoons fresh Parmesan, grated

Fresh minced parsley

Preheat the oven to 350°. Lightly spray a 9 by 13 inch rectangular baking pan with non-stick cooking spray.

Prepare lasagne noodles if they need boiling or have ready, no-cook variety. Prepare the zucchini and toss in a bowl with the broccoli and spinach.

For the Garlic Béchamel, in a 3-quart saucepan, over low heat, warm up the olive oil about one minute. Stir in the flour and cook until flour is pasty. Slowly pour in the vegetable broth, whisking all the while, and then quickly, whisk in the garlic, white wine, salt, and pepper. Whisk in the milk, stirring all the while, increase the heat, and whisk/cook until mixture thickens to a thin milkshake consistency, about 1-2 minutes. Stir in the Chevre cheese and remove from heat.

To assemble lasagne, spoon about ½ cup of marinara sauce into casserole. Lay down a layer of pasta. Smear on some more marinara, about ½ cup of béchamel, then the zucchini mix. Top with another layer of pasta. Smear on more marinara, béchamel, and the dot with the pesto, scatter on some parsley, basil, and a pinch of Italian spices. Sprinkle on about 1 cup of mozzarella. Top with another layer of pasta, then marinara, béchamel, and drop the ricotta in dollops over this layer. Top with more pasta, and use up remaining marinara, béchamel, and spices. The final layer should be: pasta, marinara, béchamel in drizzled over, pinch of spices, basil leaves, and last cup of mozzarella cheese and dusting of the Parmesan.

Bake 35-45 minutes until mixture seems hot through and through and top is bubbling slightly.

Serves 6-8

Vegetarian Cabbage Rolls

Sometimes you want an old faithful sort of recipe, but in a vegetarian revamp!

Filling

1 cup cooked brown rice

1 medium-large head green cabbage

1 cup shredded carrots

2 15 oz. cans brown lentils, drained

1 8-oz package mushrooms, chopped

¼ cup olive oil

1 small onion, chopped

Sweet Sour Sauce

1 28-oz can crushed fire-roasted tomatoes,

3 cups tomato sauce (homemade or bought)

2-3 tablespoons brown sugar

Salt and pepper to taste

1 tablespoon lemon juice

Prepare the rice as per your usual method. Core the cabbage. Boil a large pot of water. Using tongs lower the cabbage into the water. Boil for 5 minutes, rolling the cabbage to rest on a different side about halfway through. Remove cabbage from the water and drain. Cool well and then remove leaves carefully and remove the large vein in each leaf.

For the filling, heat olive oil in a large skillet and sauté onions for a few minutes and then add the mushrooms to soften a few minutes, then add the carrots, lentils, and salt; simmer on lowest heat possible for 2-3 minutes. Mash the lentils with a potato masher and then fold in the cooked rice. Continue to simmer, uncovered, until they are the consistency of moist refried beans. Remove from heat and add additional salt and pepper to taste. Remove the filling and rinse the pan briefly and then fill with the Sweet Sour Sauce ingredients including fire roasted tomatoes, tomato sauce, brown sugar, salt, and pepper. Warm up on lowest heat possible while making cabbage rolls.

To assemble cabbage rolls, place a cabbage leaf on a work surface with the wide side facing you and the sliced-out center (where the vein used to be) vertical. Bring together the split sides of the leaf and overlap. Add ¼ to 1/3 cup of filling in the bottom of the leaf (where the vein was cut out) and roll up, away from you. You'll notice that the leaf's natural curve makes this easy to do. When you finish rolling each leaf, place it in the tomato sauce, seam side down, in a single layer in the prepared skillet or pot. When the rolls are all ready and arranged in the pan, pour in enough sauce to cover the rolls. Bring to a low boil and then reduce heat, simmer on low, covered, for about 25 minutes. If sauce has thickened, heat additional sauce to pour over the rolls before serving. Or allow to cool and then store in a well-sealed container for up to three days, then reheat.

Serves 6-7

Quinoa Burgers

I use a mixture of red and white quinoa for this. These are most appealing if you match them up with pita bread and put out some falafel toppings such as tahini sauce, minced onion, pickles of various sorts, and red pickled cabbage.

In a large bowl, mix all ingredients together. Chill twenty minutes. With wet hands (or wear disposable gloves, first washed in water) shape into burgers (4 ounce) by making first into a large ball and then flattening slightly and then shaping sides to make them square sided.

Preheat oven to 350°. Line a baking sheet with parchment paper and smear with 2-3 tablespoons oil. Place burgers on baking sheet and bake 25-30 minutes until golden brown all over, turning once. Carefully remove and let cool to get more solid.

Serve on bread (pita, multi-grain), with /without hummus, shredded carrots, red onion slice and shredded romaine.

Makes 8

2 cups cooked quinoa

¼ cup shredded carrot

2 tablespoons onion, finely minced

2 tablespoons parsley, finely minced

½ cup grated white cheddar cheese, optional

2 tablespoons Parmesan cheese, optional

1 teaspoon minced garlic

½ teaspoon onion powder

¼ teaspoon pepper

¾ teaspoon salt

¾ cup breadcrumbs

3 eggs

2-3 tablespoons oil

Sweet Potato Quinoa Cutlets

Nothing beats cutlets whether they are chicken or in this case, vegetarian. These are packed with nutrition and are good for any week day meal or as holiday fare.

1/3 cup quinoa, rinsed

1/3 cup red lentils

1 2/3 cups water

Salt, pepper

1½ pounds sweet potatoes, baked

3 cups, packed chopped fresh spinach or arugula

3 ounces feta, crumbled (about ¾ cup), optional

1 tablespoon chopped fresh mint

¼ cup minced chives

2 teaspoons fresh lemon juice

1 cup panko

¼ cup vegetable oil

Combine quinoa, red lentils, water and salt to taste (about ½ teaspoon) in a saucepan and bring to a boil. Reduce heat, cover and simmer 15 to 20 minutes, until quinoa is tender and blond quinoa displays a thread, and lentils are just tender. Drain off any water remaining in the pot through a strainer, tapping strainer against the sink to remove excess water, and then return quinoa and lentils to the pot. Cover pot with a towel, then return the lid and let sit undisturbed for 15 minutes.

Skin sweet potatoes and place in a large bowl. Mash with a fork. Add spinach and mash together (I use my hands for this). Add quinoa and lentils, feta, mint, chives, lemon juice, and salt and pepper to taste. Mix together well; mixture will be moist. Preheat oven to 350°. Line a large baking sheet with parchment paper and smear pan with some olive oil.

Take up about 1/3 cup of the mixture and form into a ball (you can wet your hands to reduce sticking). Roll the ball in the panko or chickpea flour, then gently flatten into a patty.

Place on baking sheet and bake, turning once, for 25-30 minutes until golden brown on both sides. Serve with a salad and toppings, such as the usual ketchup, mustard or Greek yogurt with herbs.

Makes 10 patties

Vegetarian Black Bean Chilli

This is a gorgeous chili replete with cubes of squash, sweet potatoes along with black beans and an unbeatable spice combination.

In a large, non-stick Dutch oven style pan, over medium heat, add the olive oil and then onion; sauté the onion until lightly golden, about 10-15 minutes. Stir in and sauté the squash, sweet potato, garlic and cilantro. Season with salt and pepper and let cook about 10 minutes, over low heat, stirring often.

Stir in the water, tomatoes, tofu, ancho powder, chili and taco seasoning. Let simmer on low heat, stirring in some water to ensure it doesn't get too thick nor scorch on bottom, about 20-25 minutes. Add in the beans and cook another 15 minutes.

Fold in arugula before serving. Top with sour cream, chives, shredded cheddar cheese.

Serves 4-5

2 tablespoons olive oil

½ cup onion finely chopped

1 cup (peeled) squash cubes, about 1 inch

1 cup (peeled) sweet potatoes, about 1 inch

2 tablespoons minced cilantro

Salt, pepper

1/3 cup water or vegetable broth

1 19 ounce can crushed or ground tomatoes

1 pound package of browned tofu protein, ground up (like hamburger), optional

1-2 tablespoons cumin

1 teaspoon sweet paprika or smoked paprika

1-2 teaspoons chili powder

1 package taco seasoning, optional

1 19 ounce can of black beans (or kidney beans)

2 cups arugula

Chapter Eleven
Passover

Passover

Although there might be grumblings about 'no bread, all matzoh' by the time Passover arrives, it's also the arrival of spring, be it mid-March or early April, and Passover finally shows up! You can feel both the heaviness of winter and the spiritual fatigue of bondage the Haggadah recounts slough off. This particular holiday is a beautiful release into the light after of the gloomy darkness of winter. Passover celebrates hope and newness, and is appropriately heralded in by soft breezes, sprouting crocuses, and the return of the Canadian geese as they make their way homewards. With its rituals and timeless customs, it is part of the welcome, generic faith of spring.

Passover is a holiday that is all about careful planning and thoughtful preparation. A great time saver of mine is to freeze the entire stock pot of chicken soup since the soup and matzoh balls take time and it's an essential. Once the soup is made, I focus on making desserts (batches of Matzoh Buttercrunch as gifts, nibbling and for the Seders). Next, I do the horseradish – which is best made ahead and allowed to cure for a good week beforehand. Brisket also is delectable, made ahead and frozen. For the time right before Passover, that is when I turn my attention to the Seder plate (assembling the symbolic foods and storing them in the fridge – but they are ready when needed), chicken dishes, side dishes, and the house itself (changing dishes, fetching bridge chairs, and the Passover spring clean-up). Certainly, each household is different, but to host with some degree of serenity, it's just wise to spend some time and go step by step and freeze what you can.

In this chapter, I've given you some of my best bets for not only the Seders but throughout the Passover week that follows. (And don't forget many of the recipes in the Chicken Chapter are perfect for Passover, so check it out when preparing your Passover menu.)

Passover Morning Matzoh Brei

This beloved, traditional egg and matzoh dish is usually served with maple syrup. It's served for breakfast, brunch or a snack. All you need is a well-seasoned cast iron pan or non-stick one to make this classic

Break matzoh into coarse pieces with your hands. Place in a large bowl and cover with milk and allow to soak 10 minutes. If the milk seems insufficient, add a bit of warm water as required (different brands of matzoh soak up liquid at different rates). Mix in beaten eggs and salt and sugar to make a lumpy batter - gloppy enough to spoon into a pan to fry.

In a large non-stick skillet over medium heat, add a tablespoon or so of butter or margarine. Using a large ladle, spoon about ½-1 cup of matzoh brei batter to the pan (or in what size pancakes you prefer).

Fry lightly on one side, as a pancake and turn once. Alternatively, for a large matzoh brie (one large pancakes), use an 8 or 9 inch non-stick skillet, and make several large matzoh brei(s), serving one per person. When preparing the larger version, once batter is added to the pan, reduce heat to low and let batter set, much like an omelette. Carefully turn and allow top side to lightly brown.

Serves 1-2

4 sheets matzoh

1½ cups warm milk or warm water

6 eggs

1/8 teaspoon salt

1 tablespoon sugar

Unsalted butter

Maple syrup, jam

Passover Granola

No oats, no sesame seeds, but still, a delicious Passover granola. If you don't have farfel, use the equivalent in broken up egg and plain matzoh.

1¼ cup vegetable oil

¼ cup Passover maple table syrup

¼ cup warm honey

6-7 cups matzoh farfel lightly toasted in the oven

½ cup chopped walnuts

1 cup slivered almonds

1½ cups shredded coconut

1½ cups raisins

½ cup each dates (slivered, chopped), cranberries, dried cherries

1/3 cup brown sugar

1/8 teaspoon salt

1 package Passover vanilla powder, optional

½ teaspoon cinnamon

Preheat oven to 300°. Mix dry ingredients (excluding dried fruit) together in a large bowl.

In a small saucepan combine oil and honey and maple syrup. Heat over low heat until mixture is warm enough to blend together.

Pour wet mix into dry ingredients and mix thoroughly, adding in vanilla powder as you mix.

Spread mixture into two or three large baking pans and slow bake or toast in low oven for one hour and ten minutes. Stir every ten or fifteen minutes. Granola is done when golden brown. Remove from oven and stir in dried fruit.

Cool completely in pans, then store in an airtight container and refrigerate.

Makes 10-12 cups

Passover Paradise Haroses

This delectable haroses is the symbolic "mortar" used to sandwich pieces of matzoh together at the Seder table. It features fresh apples, cranberries, raisins and cinnamon and (for allergy peeps) no nuts! This is more like a relish or compote; it's bright, sweet and tart and a wonderful offering with roast chicken or turkey on Shabbat as well as during Passover. One taste and you will see why it's called 'Paradise haroses'.

Place all ingredients in a medium saucepan. Over low-medium heat, cook the fruit slowly until the apples soften and cranberries pop open. Stir, ensuring mixture does not burn on bottom. You may have to lower heat.

After it is cooked down and is thicker, adjust tartness to taste with more orange juice and sugar if you wish - or, if it seems too thick, add a touch more water or orange juice. Cool well. Refrigerate after it cools down. Serve cold or room temperature. (Some of this is used on the Seder plate and a side dish may be offered with the main meal.)

Makes about 1¾ cups

2 cups fresh cranberries

½ cup dried cherries

¼ cup dried cranberries

1/3 cup yellow raisins

2 cups coarsely chopped apples

½ cup sugar

¾ cup water

½ cup water or orange juice

2 tablespoons sweet red wine

½ teaspoon cinnamon

Passover Matzoh Meal Kugel

This matzoh-based kugel is packed with goodies as well as being unique, moist and a welcome change of pace. It's one of those side dishes that will become one of your signature Passover recipes.

2 cups matzoh farfel

4 cups broken matzoh, plain or egg (or a combo)

2-3 cups hot water or hot vegetable or chicken stock

¼ cup vegetable oil

1 cup celery, finely minced

1 cup carrots, shredded

1 small onion, finely diced

½ cup red pepper, finely minced

1 cup mushrooms, finely minced (optional)

2 garlic cloves, finely minced

1 teaspoon garlic powder

1 teaspoon onion powder

1 teaspoon paprika

Salt, pepper

4 eggs

Preheat oven to 350°. Oil a 4-quart casserole or baking dish with vegetable oil. A 9-inch quiche pan with removable bottom is perfect. Place the pan on a parchment paper lined baking sheet.

In a large bowl, cover the matzoh and farfel with hot broth, using only two cups until you see how much more liquid is required. Sufficient broth is required to soften the matzoh and farfel without flooding it into a paste. You want it mushy. Let the mixture stand five minutes and then stir a bit and then add more liquid if mixture is not yet softened and break up the pieces of matzoh.

In a large skillet, over medium heat, add the oil and sauté the celery, carrots, onion, red pepper, and mushrooms in oil, adding in a touch more oil and small amounts of water to allow vegetables to soften and brown slightly, 8-12 minutes. Stir in the garlic and cook another minute or so.

Stir the vegetables into the matzoh mixture. Let cool 10 minutes and then blend the eggs, garlic powder, onion powder, paprika, salt and pepper and eggs and stir. Taste and adjust salt if more is required. Spoon the mixture into the prepared baking dish or casserole and bake until nicely browned, about 35-45 minutes.

Serves 8-10

Three-Level Kugel

Sometimes you need something homey but dressed to impress and tri-level kugel is just the thing. Perfect anytime but especially glamourous at Passover, this is also a great vegetarian offering because it's one of those centerpiece side dishes that brings Oh's and Ah's.

Broccoli Layer

1 pound broccoli, cooked, chopped fine

3 eggs

½ cup matzoh meal

1½ teaspoon garlic powder

¾ teaspoon salt

3/8 teaspoon pepper

Carrot Squash Layer

2 cups carrots, shredded

1 cup butternut squash, cooked and mashed

¼ cup brown sugar

1 egg

1½ cup matzoh meal

½ teaspoon salt

¼ teaspoon cinnamon

1/3 cup orange juice

Cauliflower Layer

¼ cup canola oil

½ cup diced onion

1 pound cauliflower, cooked, finely chopped

3 eggs

1 cup matzoh meal

½ teaspoon salt

¼ teaspoon pepper

Line a 10-inch spring-form pan with parchment paper (bottom and sides). Spray with non-stick cooking spray. Preheat oven to 350°. Place pan on a parchment paper lined baking sheet.

Prepare first layer by cooking broccoli and then combining with rest of ingredients (for that layer) in a bowl. Spread in spring-form pan. For the second layer, in a bowl, blend the carrots, with squash, sugar, egg, matzoh meal, salt, cinnamon and orange juice. Gently spread over broccoli layer.

For the third layer, prepare cauliflower. In a small skillet, heat the oil and sauté the onion until lightly cooked and golden. Place with cauliflower in a large bowl and stir in the eggs, matzoh meal, salt and pepper. Gently spread this over carrot-squash mixture.

Bake 50-60 minutes or until a skewer inserted in center comes out clean. Cool 15 minutes before serving.

8-10 servings

Famous Sweet Potato Molded Kugel

A potato kugel is a perfect side dish staple for Passover. I often use a glass Bundt pan for this recipe as it enables me to see the kugel browning as it bakes making it easy to tell when it's done. Any similar ring mold is fine as you will be unmolding this for a pretty presentation that also ensures easy, elegant servings by the slice.

2½ pounds sweet potatoes

1 medium onion, finely shredded

2 tablespoons finely minced parsley

Salt, pepper

1/3 cup vegetable oil

4 eggs

Use a ring mold such as a tube or angel food cake pan. Generously spray a 10-inch round baking mold with non-stick cooking spray or smear with vegetable oil and line inner sides and bottom with parchment paper. Place on a parchment paper-lined baking sheet.

Parboil potatoes. Put them in a large pot and barely cover with cold water. Bring to a boil, reduce heat to low, and let simmer for 5 minutes. Time everything exactly; for this recipe it really is important to obtain best results. Remove and cover with cold water. Preheat oven to 350°.

Using a hand grater, shred potatoes. Put them in a large bowl and then toss with minced onions, parsley, salt, pepper, oil and eggs. Spray a 12-cup angel or tube cake pan with non-stick cooking spray. Spoon the potato batter into the pan. Bake until top is nicely browned, 35-45 minutes. Invert before serving.

Serves 6-10

Passover Sweet Potato Kugel

This is a savory kugel, although it's made with sweet potatoes. It's bright and colorful, a beautiful counterpoint to the brisket and chicken dishes on the traditional Passover table.

Preheat oven to 350°. Generously spray a 4-quart casserole dish with non-stick cooking spray or smear with oil.

Grate the sweet potatoes and place in a large bowl. Blend in the onions, scallions, olive oil, eggs, flour, salt and pepper. Spoon into the pan.

Bake until top is gently browned, 45 minutes.

Serves 6-8

4 large sweet potatoes, peeled

1 medium onion finely, minced

3 scallions, finely diced

¼ cup light olive oil

5 eggs

½ cup flour

1½ teaspoons salt

¼ teaspoon pepper

Passover Carrot Kugel Pudding

This is sweet, but not overly so. Being orange and spicy, it's a nice counterpoint to brisket and roast chicken or duck.

3 cups grated carrots

3 eggs

1 cup matzoh cake meal

1 teaspoon salt

¼ teaspoon cinnamon

Zest of one orange, finely minced

½ cup brown sugar

1/3 cup vegetable oil

Preheat oven to 350°. Spray a 9-inch baking dish with non-stick cooking spray or smear with oil.

Prepare the carrots. Separate eggs and whisk the whites, in a mixing bowl, with a pinch of salt, until soft peaks form. In a large bowl, hand whisk the cake meal, salt and cinnamon. Add in the orange zest, oil, egg yolks and carrots and blend. Fold in the egg whites, gently but thoroughly.

Spoon mixture into prepared pan and place on a baking sheet.

Bake until just set, 35-40 minutes. Cool to warm before serving.

Serves 6-8

Spinach Kale and Zucchini Kugel

I like recipes that 'get the job done' so one that fuses tradition (a kugel) with nutrition (healthy greens) and flavor has (for me) real star power. A great side dish and something especially apropos at Sukkot as well as Passover. If you use regular kale for this, remove the tougher spines before cooking the kale.

Preheat oven to 350°. Spray a 3-quart casserole with non-stick cooking spray.

In a medium saucepan, filled with one cup of water, cook spinach, drain and chop. Repeat for the kale. In a large bowl, toss the spinach, kale, zucchini, scallions, eggs, oil, matzoh meal, spices, parsley and garlic. Pack into prepared mold.

Bake until kugel is slightly puffy, 35-40 minutes.

Serves 8

1 package fresh baby spinach, washed

1 package baby kale, washed

2 small zucchini, shredded and drained

1 carrot, shredded

3 scallions, diced

4 eggs

2 tablespoons vegetable oil

½ cup matzoh meal

½ teaspoon oregano

¼ teaspoon basil

2 tablespoons fresh minced parsley

½ teaspoon garlic powder

Passover Turkey Stuffing

Stuffing without the turkey is still wonderful, but with a Passover turkey, this Pesach-stuffing, replete with savory carrots and onions and some sweet cranberries, is a winning offering! My best recipe for turkey is the Brined Hanukkah Roast Turkey found in the Chicken & Turkey Chapter. It's suitable for Passover, providing you match it with this Passover-delicious stuffing.

5 cups broken matzoh

1 cup matzoh meal

2-3 cups hot water or vegetable or chicken stock

¼ cup vegetable oil

1 cup celery, finely minced

1 cup shredded carrots

1 small onion, finely diced

½ cup red pepper, finely minced

1 cup mushrooms, finely minced (optional)

2 garlic cloves finely minced

1 teaspoon garlic powder

1 teaspoon onion powder

1 teaspoon paprika

½ teaspoon turkey or poultry seasoning

Salt, pepper

4 eggs

½ cup cranberries, optional

½ cup chopped apples, optional

Preheat oven to 350°. Oil a 4-quart casserole or baking dish with vegetable oil.

In a large bowl, cover the matzoh with hot broth, using only two cups until you see how much more liquid is required. Enough broth is required to soften the matzoh without flooding it into a paste; you want it mushy. Let the mixture stand five minutes and then stir a bit and then add more liquid if mixture is not yet softened and break up the pieces of matzoh.

In a large skillet, over medium heat, add the oil and sauté the celery, carrots, onion, red pepper, and mushrooms in oil, adding in a touch more oil and small amounts of water to allow vegetables to soften and brown slightly, 8-12 minutes. Stir in the garlic and cook another minute or so.

Stir the vegetables into the matzoh mixture. Let cool 10 minutes and then blend the eggs, garlic powder, onion powder, paprika, poultry seasoning salt and pepper and eggs and stir. Fold in the cranberries and apples. Taste and adjust salt if more is required. Spoon the mixture into the prepared baking dish or casserole and bake until nicely browned, about 35-45 minutes. Scoop out or cut to serve with main dish.

Serves 8-10

Roasted Mediterranean Vegetables

This is so classic, but so wonderful, quick and easy!

Preheat oven to 375°. Have a 6-quart oven casserole or roasting dish ready.

Prepare vegetables. Place in casserole and drizzle with oil (just to coat vegetables nicely), and season with salt and pepper.

Roast until the vegetables are softened and browned around the edges, about 45 – 55 minutes, or as required.

Serves 6-8

4 red-skinned or Yukon Gold potatoes, cut in large wedges

2 Bermuda onions, cut in wedges

1 red onion, sliced thickly

1 large bulb of garlic, separated and peeled

1 medium eggplant, peeled and in large cubes

2 medium yellow zucchinis in 1-inch chunks

Olive oil

Salt, pepper

Passover Vegetable Mini Kugels

These are more mini kugels or 'kuggelins' but unique and tasty, regardless of nomenclature. Formed in patties and lightly fried or oven baked, they are great vegetable-based stand-ins for latkes.

1/3 cup vegetable oil

1/3 cup chopped green pepper

1 cup chopped onion

½ cup chopped celery

1½ cups grated carrots

1 10 ounce package chopped spinach

3 eggs

1½ teaspoons salt

1/8 teaspoon pepper

¾ cup matzoh meal

Generously smear a 12-cup muffin tin with a bit of the oil and set aside.

In a medium skillet, sauté the green pepper, onion, celery and carrots until softened, about 5-8 minutes. Place spinach in a large bowl and microwave (5 minutes on High) to cook and then drain and chop.

In a large bowl, combine the sautéed vegetables, the spinach, then eggs, salt, pepper and matzoh meal. Spoon equal amounts of this batter into the prepared muffin tin wells. Bake until just set, about 45 minutes. Allow to stand 10 minutes before serving.

To fry as you would potato latkes, spoon small amounts of batter into hot oil and fry, a few minutes each side.

Serves 8-10

Matzoh, Mushroom and Onion Kugel

The trick here is to brown the matzoh in the oven first – for more flavor.

Preheat oven to 350°. Lightly grease a 9 by 13 inch casserole or roasting dish and set aside.

Break up matzoh boards coarsely and place on a large baking sheet, or two, and bake, watching carefully, to brown the matzoh. Cool to almost room temperature. Meanwhile, in a large skillet, heat the oil a minute or two. Over low heat sauté the onions and mushrooms until softened but not brown and crisp, about 7-10 minutes. Cool.

Place matzoh in a large bowl and cover with chicken stock and water, as required, to soften matzoh. Let stand 5 minutes and drain. Add the sautéed vegetables to the matzoh, along with the eggs and seasonings and mix well. Spoon into pre-pared dish.

Bake until set and slightly browned, about 45-60 minutes.

Serves 8-10

10 matzoh sheets

2 medium onions, diced

½ pound fresh mushrooms, well washed and sliced

¼ cup vegetable oil

1 cup chicken stock

1 teaspoon salt

1 teaspoon paprika

¼ teaspoon pepper

½ teaspoon garlic powder

1 cup water

Passover Caponata

This is the simplest, sunniest dish you can imagine. You layer on the ingredients – don't bother stirring, just let it slow roast and then dip in.

1 large egg plant, washed, trimmed, diced into 1-inch cubes

1 small lemon washed, thinly sliced

4 medium zucchini, washed, trimmed and sliced into ½ inch slices

½ cup pitted or pimento stuffed green olives

½ cup pitted black olives, sliced

½ bunch parsley, fined minced

½ teaspoon dry Italian spices

1 28 ounce can ground or diced tomatoes

Salt, pepper

¼ cup red wine

4 cloves of garlic, finely minced

2 tablespoons lemon juice

1/3 cup extra virgin olive oil

Preheat oven to 350°.

Add everything to a 4-5 quart Dutch oven in order given. Cover and roast, 2-3 hours until vegetables are softened and cooked down, reducing oven temperature to 325° midway. Alternatively, you can start at 325° and cook it 3-4 hours without temperature adjustment.

Adjust seasonings. Serve hot or cold

Serves 6-8

Golden Asparagus Artichoke Matzoh Quiche

This is a very spring-like approach to matzoh brei. Minced vegetables in a matzoh brei base make this a welcome change of pace. You can also opt to add some cheese, making this a dairy dish variation.

Steam the asparagus. Cool, then drain and dice. Mince the artichokes and mix in a bowl with the asparagus.

Line a ceramic (no removable bottom) quiche pan with a smear of margarine and a dusting of matzoh meal. Place on a parchment lined baking sheet.

In a medium skillet, heat the butter or oil and sauce the scallions or onions to soften, but not color, about 10 minutes. Preheat oven to 350°.

Meanwhile, in a large bowl, crumble the matzoh sheets and then cover the matzoh meal with warm water (just to barely cover the matzoh) and let stand 3 minutes. Drain excess water. Blend eggs into the soaked matzoh, and then add in the vegetables; season with salt and pepper. (Add cheese now if using).

Spoon mixture out into quiche pan. Brush top with some olive oil. Bake until bubbling and slightly golden on top, about 30-40 minutes.

Serve warm or cold. Serves 4

3 tablespoons olive oil

8 medium spears asparagus

3 artichoke hearts cooked, finely minced

½ cup finely minced scallions

5 matzoh sheets

6 eggs

Salt, pepper

1 cup grated cheddar cheese or cottage, optional

Famous Passover Matzoh Stuffing

This savoury stuffing is too good to save for Passover! Use it in chicken or turkey or pat it in a casserole as a side dish much like a stuffing. If you bake it in a square pan and let it bake longer, you will get another dish: matzoh kugel, which is as delectable as the perfect Passover side.

2 cups matzoh farfel, or broken matzoh

4 cups broken matzoh, plain or egg (or a combo)

2-3 cups hot water or hot vegetable or chicken stock

¼ cup vegetable oil

1 cup celery, finely minced

1 cup carrots, shredded

1 small onion, finely diced

½ cup green pepper, finely minced

1 cup mushrooms, finely minced (optional)

1 garlic clove, finely minced

1 teaspoon garlic powder

1 teaspoon onion powder

Salt, pepper

4 eggs

Preheat oven to 350°. Oil a 4-quart casserole or baking dish with vegetable oil.

In a large bowl, cover the matzoh and farfel with hot broth, putting in 2 cups first until you see how much more liquid is required. You need enough broth to soften the matzoh and farfel without flooding it into a paste. Let it stand and stir a bit and then add more liquid if mixture is not yet softened.

In a large skillet, over medium heat, sauté the celery, carrots, onion, green pepper, and mushrooms in oil, adding in a touch more oil and small amounts of water to allow vegetables to soften and brown slightly, 8-12 minutes. Stir in the garlic and cook another minute or so.

Stir the vegetables into the matzoh mixture. Let cool 10 minutes and then blend the eggs, garlic powder, onion powder, salt and pepper and eggs and stir. Taste and adjust salt if more is required.

Serves 8-10

Extra Crispy Passover Chicken Cutlets

Don't you love when a substitution becomes better than your original method or ingredients? Matzoh meal makes a terrific coating mix for anything chicken cutlets (or turkey filets or fish). Together with the potato starch (instead of flour as one would usually use when it is not Passover) this coating results in crunchy, golden chicken cutlets or fillets that are as good as a snack or appetizer as they are a main dish.

Lay out a large sheet of wax or parchment paper to work on. Put the prepared chicken strips on one side of this work surface, then a shallow bowl with the potato starch in it. In a larger bowl, mix the matzoh meal, salt, pepper, garlic and onion powder together and have this nearby. In a medium bowl, prepare the eggs (beating just to blend as the egg coating). What is required is an 'assembly line' to work with of chicken, potato starch, eggs, and last, the seasoned matzoh meal.

Dust the chicken strips lightly with salt and pepper. Dredge the strips lightly and shake off, in the potato starch. Then lower the chicken strips into the beaten eggs, then dip and press in seasoned matzoh meal.

Using a large skillet, heat oil (up to ¼ of sides) to 350°. Fry a few pieces of chicken at a time, turning once, until well browned on each side - adjust heat as required. Drain well. Serve warm or cold.

Serves 4-6

2 pounds skinless chicken breasts, cut into strips

1 cup potato starch, approximately

Salt, pepper

3 cups matzoh meal

1 tablespoon salt

1 teaspoon black pepper

1 tablespoon garlic powder

1 teaspoon onion powder

4 eggs

Vegetable oil

Quinoa Sweet and Sour Meatballs

A Passover version of the classic meat-based sweet-and-sour meatballs.

Quinoa Meatballs

2 cups cooked quinoa

¼ cup shredded carrot

2 tablespoons onion, finely minced

2 tablespoons parsley, finely minced

1 teaspoon minced garlic

½ teaspoon onion powder

¼ teaspoon pepper

¾ teaspoon salt

¾ cup matzoh meal

3 eggs

2-3 tablespoons vegetable oil

Sweet and Sour Sauce

½ can jellied cranberry sauce

½ cup grape jam

¾ cup ketchup

¼ cup brown sugar

2 teaspoons fresh lemon juice

½ cup ginger ale

¼ cup water

¼ - ½ teaspoon citric acid or sour salt, optional

In a large bowl, mix all ingredients for the meatballs together. Chill twenty minutes.

For the Sweet and Sour Sauce, in a medium saucepan, mix together the cranberry sauce, grape jam ketchup, brown sugar, lemon juice, ginger-ale, water and citric acid and heat over low heat while preparing meatballs. Preheat oven to 350°. Line a large baking sheet with parchment paper and smear with 2-3 tablespoons olive oil.

Shape the quinoa mixture into 1-inch balls. Place on baking sheet and bake until browned, 20-25 minutes. Remove and place in Sweet and Sour Sauce and cook on low heat for 30-60 minutes.

Serves 5-6

Sweet Potato Quinoa Burgers

A non-Passover version of these is in the Vegetarian Chapter. Here, matzoh meal steps in for the breadcrumbs. You can, if you prefer a non-dairy version of this dish, simply omit the cheese.

In a large bowl, mix all ingredients together. Chill a few hours (if you have time, but it is still ok if not). Shape into burgers (4 ounce). In a large skillet, add some oil and heat to medium high. Fry a few at a time 5-10 minutes. Carefully remove and let cool to get more solid.

Serve on bread (pita, multi-grain), with /without hummus, shredded carrots, red onion slice and shredded romaine.

Makes 8

2 cups cooked quinoa

¼ cup shredded carrot

2 tablespoons onion, finely minced

2 tablespoons parsley, finely minced

1 teaspoon minced garlic

½ teaspoon onion powder

¼ teaspoon pepper

¾ teaspoon salt

¾ cup matzoh meal

3 eggs

Vegetable oil for frying

Stuffed Passover Brisket

This is a triumph, not only because it revamps an old favorite, but makes it elegant and different which makes it perfect for the holidays but especially so for Passover. If you like the idea but prefer your own seasonings, use the stuffing recipe and the technique, but feel free to recreate this in your favorite family recipe. That way you will have your tradition and a new one combined.

Matzoh Kugel Stuffing

1 cup matzoh meal

4 eggs

¼ cup vegetable oil

¼ cup water

1 teaspoon salt

1/8 teaspoon pepper

½ teaspoon garlic powder

1 teaspoon onion powder

Stuffing

All of the matzoh kugel

¼ cup vegetable oil

2 cups finely chopped celery

2 cups chopped mushrooms

2 cups finely chopped carrots

1 medium onion, finely chopped

2 eggs

½ cup chicken broth or water

Brisket

1 4-5 pound brisket

Salt, pepper, garlic powder, onion powder, paprika

1 large onion, thinly sliced

1 garlic bulb, separated into cloves (but not peeled)

1 cup red wine

¼ cup cola

½ cup ketchup

½ cup beef broth

Preheat oven to 350°.

For the Matzoh Kugel, spray a 9-inch square pan with non-stick cooking spray or lightly brush with oil. In a medium bowl, mix the matzoh meal, the eggs, oil, water, salt, pepper, garlic powder, and onion powder to make a thick mixture. Pour or spoon stuffing mixture into pan. Bake until top is barely golden and mixture is set, about 30-40 minutes. Let cool.

Meanwhile for the Stuffing, in a large non-stick skillet, heat the remaining 3 tablespoons oil and add the celery, mushroom, carrots, and onion. Sauté on lowest heat until softened, about 15-25 minutes.

Once you can handle the baked matzoh kugel, grate it or dice it fine. Place it in a large bowl. Add in the sautéed vegetables, two eggs and chicken broth (or water) to make a mushy stuffing mixture. (If it seems dry, add another egg and a bit more broth or water)

Preheat oven to 325°.

For the Brisket, slit to make a pocket or slice horizontally in half (the latter method is easier to work with). Spoon the stuffing in the pocket or if you've slit the meat across in half, spread two-thirds of the stuffing mixture onto the meat. Press down the top half of the meat or if you stuffed the pocket, press the open end together.

Some will leak out but it's fine. Alternatively, you can use kitchen twine and tie the brisket up. Place remaining stuffing in large baking dish. Place brisket on top of the extra stuffing. Season it liberally with salt, pepper, garlic powder, onion powder and paprika (go easy on the salt but then more pepper; use a good 1-2 tablespoon of other spices). Top with the sliced onions. Around the side, add the garlic cloves, wine, cola, ketchup and beef broth.

Roast the brisket 4-6 hours, basting every so often with pan juices (add more water if you need more liquid) and take the foil off the top the last hour. Once it's done, refrigerate overnight.

The next day (of serving), slice the brisket thinly and place the slices in the broth (stuffing that has leaked out can stay in roasting pan). Roast slowly, at 300° until thoroughly tender, 2-4 hours.

Serves 8-12

Chapter Twelve
A Jewish Baking Sampler

This is a mini chapter or 'just a taste' of baking since the sequel to this cookbook is a whole new book on Jewish baking! There's simply too much great baking to include in a cooking book on Jewish food. It deserves it's own book. (There is also my first and classic cookbook A Treasury of Jewish Holiday Baking to consider. But there are twelve original tribes of Israel and for that reason, and also because a book on Jewish food would be (to me) incomplete without at least a mention of some of my own special baking recipe, I am delighted to offer you a baking sampler. Here are five of my favorite classic recipes to start you off. And stay tuned, for the baking sequel of this cooking book!

Easy Friday Night Challah

This is one of my easiest challah recipes that suits beginners or pros and can be made in the bread machine (mixing it, not to bake it in), mixer and dough hook or by hand. It's fragrant, moist and homey and remains one of my own favorite, go-to challah recipes.

Line a baking sheet with parchment paper.

In a mixer bowl, add the water and yeast and 1 cup of the flour. Then add the salt, sugar, eggs, honey, oil and most of the rest of the flour. Mix to blend, and then knead with a dough hook on slow speed of mixer to form a soft dough, 8-10 minutes, dusting in flour as required to make a soft, elastic dough.

Shape dough into a ball and place dough in a lightly greased bowl and place bowl in a plastic bag and seal loosely. Let rise until almost doubled, about 45-90 minutes. Gently deflate gently.

Divide dough in three and form into three strands. Braid dough and place on parchment line baking sheet. Brush with egg wash and sprinkle with sesame seeds. Insert baking sheet into a large, clear, plastic bag. Let rise until puffy and almost doubled in bulk, 45-60 minutes.

Preheat oven to 350°. Place bread in oven and let bake until well browned, about 27-30 minutes; 35-40 minutes for a loaf style bread.

Makes one large loaf

1¼ cups warm water

4½ teaspoons instant yeast

2½ teaspoons salt

1/3 cup sugar

3 eggs

2 tablespoons honey

1/3 cup vegetable oil

4½ - 5 cups bread flour

Finishing Touches

1 egg

Sesame seeds

Montreal Bagels

You can wait to visit Montreal or depend on Canadian relatives to tote some over the border (if you're stateside) or just try this authentic bagel recipe yourself. These are smaller, sweeter and more rustic than the more familiar New York Style bagel. I've spent years perfecting this recipe, visiting and watching bagel makers at work - assessing techniques and the ingredients used in the many famous Montreal bagel landmarks such as The Bagel Factory on St. Viateur and the Fairmont Bagel Factory.

1¾ cups warm water

2½ teaspoons instant yeast

5 tablespoons sugar

2 tablespoons beaten egg

3 tablespoons oil

1 tablespoon malt powder

1½ teaspoons salt, optional

4½ - 5 cups bread flour

1½ cups sesame seed or poppy seeds

Kettle Water

6 quarts water

1/3 cup honey

In a mixer bowl, whisk together the water and yeast, and let stand a couple of minutes, allowing yeast to dissolve. Briskly whisk in sugar, beaten egg, vegetable oil, malt and fold in most of the flour. Knead on slow speed 10-12 minutes to form a stiff, smooth dough, begin kneading, 10-12 minutes, adding additional flour as required. Cover with a tea towel and let rest ten minutes. Preheat oven to 450°.

Line one large baking sheet with a kitchen towel, the other with parchment paper. Fill a large pot two-thirds full of water and add the honey and salt. Bring water to a gentle boil. Meanwhile, divide in 12 sections and form into 10-inch strips. Form these into bagel rings and place on cookie sheet. Let rise 12-16 minutes until bagels are slightly puffed up.

Boil bagels about 1½ minutes each, turning over once. Place on towel-lined sheet first to dry out. Then sprinkle very generously with sesame or poppy seeds (Montreal Bagels are more seeded than regular bagels). Place on parchment lined sheet.

Place in oven; reduce heat to 425°. Bake until done, about 15-22 minutes, turning bagels over once when they are just about done.

Makes 12

Moist and Majestic New Year's Honey Cake

I like a New Year's honey cake to be extra moist and sweet, as good on the day of baking as it is days later. This one is queen of the realm - rich with honey, nicely spiced, in a word, majestic - in taste and stature. I went through many variations and tasting sessions until I was satisfied with this definitive cake. One tester gave the ultimate compliment, saying "this one is worth the price of the book".

Very Important Baker's Tip:

If cake seems done but still seems a bit wobbly in center, lower the oven temperature and give it 10-20 more minutes. This is very important – give the cake the amount of baking it needs.

Preheat oven to 350°. Line the bottom and sides of a 10-inch angel food cake pan lightly greased parchment paper, cut to fit. Stack two baking sheets together and line the top one with parchment paper. Place cake pan on that (this prevents the bottom from browning too quickly)

In a large bowl or large food processor, blend together the flour, baking powder, baking soda, salt, cinnamon, cloves and allspice. Make a well in the center, and add oil, honey, white sugar, brown sugars, eggs, vanilla, coffee, orange juice and rye or whisky. Blend well, making sure that no ingredients are stuck to the bottom. This is a thin batter.

Spoon batter into prepared pan and sprinkle top of cake (s) evenly with almonds. Place cake pan on baking sheet.

Bake until cake tests done, that is, it springs back when you gently touch the cake center, 55-65 minutes.

Let cake stand fifteen minutes before removing from pan.

* If you prefer not to use the whisky, replace it with orange juice or coffee.

3½ cups all-purpose flour

1 tablespoon baking powder

1 teaspoon baking soda

½ teaspoon salt

1 tablespoon cinnamon

½ teaspoon cloves

¼ teaspoon allspice

1 cup vegetable oil

1 cup honey

1½ cups white sugar

½ cup brown sugar

3 eggs

1 teaspoon pure vanilla extract

1 cup warm coffee or strong tea

¾ cup orange juice

¼ cup rye or whisky *

½ cup slivered or sliced almonds, optional

Legendary Matzoh Buttercrunch

This recipe almost needs no introduction. I created it in the mid-'80s and it went onto become a sensation that everyone makes (even Martha Stewart!). It's a Passover must.

4-6 unsalted matzoh boards or sheets

1 cup unsalted butter or unsalted Passover margarine

1 cup light brown sugar

¾ cup chocolate chips or semi-sweet chocolate, coarsely chopped

Preheat oven to 350°. Line doubled up, rimmed cookie sheets completely with foil. Cover bottom of pan with baking parchment - on top of foil. This is very important as mixture becomes sticky during baking. Line bottom of pan evenly with matzoh boards, cutting extra pieces of matzoh, as required, fitting any spaces on the cookie sheet as evenly as possible.

Combine butter and brown sugar in a 3-quart, heavy-bottomed, saucepan. Cook over medium heat, stirring constantly, until mixture comes to a boil. Continue cooking 3 more minutes, stirring constantly. Remove from heat and spoon or pour over matzoh.

Bake 15 minutes, checking every few minutes to make sure mixture is not burning. If it seems to be browning too quickly, remove from oven, lower heat to 325°. and return to oven for remaining time.

Remove from oven and sprinkle matzoh boards immediately with chopped chocolate or chips. Let stand 5 minutes, then spread melted chocolate over matzoh. While still warm cut into squares or odd shapes. Chill in refrigerator until set. This makes a good gift. You can also serve it in confectioners' paper cups as a candy.

Serves: Never makes enough!

Grandma's Best Sour Cream Marble Cake

There is something so simple and satisfying about a marble cake, it's no wonder it is a favourite in the Jewish kitchen. Other cakes are fancier, frosted, or just plain glitzier but marble cake always holds in own. Moister than a pound cake, richer than a quick bread, this is the perfect sweet to have around over the weekend. Dusting the pan with demerara sugar is optional, but it makes a wonderful taste and texture sensation

Preheat the oven to 350°. Line an 8 by 4 ½ inch loaf pan with parchment paper. Smear the paper with butter and then dust on the demerara sugar (reserving some for the top of the cake). Stack two baking sheets together and line the top one with parchment paper. Place loaf pan on it (this cake browns easily and the pan treatment prevents that).

Prepare chocolate paste by placing cocoa and butter in a small bowl and blending well, adding a drop or more of hot water if mixture is too stiff.

For cake, in a mixer bowl, blend the butter with the sugar until light and fluffy, scraping bowl often. Blend in eggs and stir in vanilla, almond extract, milk, sour cream and orange zest and blend well. In a separate bowl, whisk together the flour, baking soda, powder and salt and add to the wet ingredients.

Remove one-third of batter to a smaller bowl. Stir chocolate paste into this to make a chocolate batter. Spoon alternating portions of white and chocolate batter into prepared pan. Using a knife, swirl the batter to marbleize.

Bake 55-60 minutes until cake tests done. Cake should be lightly browned on top and spring back when lightly pressed. Let cool 15-20 minutes in pan before inverting onto wire rack.

Serves 8-10

Chocolate Paste

3 tablespoons cocoa
3 tablespoons unsalted melted butter

Cake

Butter for pan
3 tablespoons demerara sugar
½ cup unsalted butter, room temperate
1 cup and 2 tablespoons sugar
2 eggs
1 tablespoon pure vanilla extract
¼ teaspoon pure almond extract
3 tablespoons milk
½ cup sour cream
Zest of one orange, finely minced, optional
1½ cup plus 2 tablespoons all-purpose flour
½ teaspoon baking soda
2 teaspoons baking powder
¼ teaspoon salt

Acknowledgements

Cookbooks, especially comprehensive ones like this one is, depend on the efforts, generosity and palate of others to bring it out into the world. This book is no exception. I've been particularly blessed to have a team of volunteer testers who have ensured each and every crumb in each and every recipe in this book is perfection: perfection in taste, hopefully but also in the fine-tuning of the editorial component of each recipe.

I'd like to acknowledge this incredible group of people for their invaluable contributions to this book:

Jan Hirsch, Senior Editor

Michele Meiner, Proof-reader.

Stephanie Sedgwick, Proof-reader, Editor

Recipe Testers

Lori Balthazar

Karen Brenker

Mary Bohner

Lynn Burton

Darleen Chicoine

Wendy Christy

Diane DiVittorio

Amy Fink

Judith Fuchs

Sherri Holcman

Joyce Landes

Alix Langer

JoAnna Lamprecht

Rhona Levitan

Diane Loeffen

Sivan Galor

Danielle Lubashevsky

Sharon Grossman

Marilyn Hoffman

Joyce Leitman

Alana Lesueur

Marla Marcus and Allen Marcus

Susan Hatch

Caryn Netter

Stephanie Sedgwick

Brondell Shapiro

Judy Solomon

Caryn Stellman

Amy Stromberg

Susan Sussman

Peggy Carroll-Tornberg

Pilar Torres

Eric Weinstein

Catherine Wiese

Tina Ujlaki

Lois Urkowitz

Free Bonus Recipe Offer from Marcy Goldman's Betterbaking.com

Two Months All Recipe Access to Betterbaking.com!

To obtain your free two guest months of Betterbaking.com simply email an electronic copy of your purchase of *The Newish Jewish Cookbook*. Betterbaking.com, launched in 1997, is my website and home to over 2500 of my original recipes online, including Jewish food, other cuisines and baking. You will also receive my monthly newsletter with the new recipes of the month. If you are already a BB subscriber, I am pleased to extend your subscription!

Index of Recipe Titles
(by chapter)